The New Retirement Paradigm

Breaking Free from the Old Rules

Douglas B Sims, PhD

Printed in the United States of America.

For more information, or to book an event, contact:
dsims@simsassociates.net

Book design by DB Sims
Cover design by DB Sims

ISBN – Paperback: 979-8-9913292-7-9
ISBN – eBook: 979-8-9913292-6-2

Font cover picture is from Pixabay

First Edition: September 2024

Disclaimer

I am not a Certified Financial Planner (CFP), a retirement expert, or a professional selling or advising on any retirement or savings strategy. The information provided is for informational purposes only and should not be considered as financial advice. For personalized financial guidance, please consult with a qualified financial advisor.

Douglas B Sims

Table of Contents

Douglas B Sims

Acknowledgements

First and foremost, I want to thank my family, whose unwavering support and patience have been my greatest source of strength. To my wife, whose encouragement and understanding kept me grounded through the ups and downs of our lives and this project—thank you for always having my back. To my kids, for reminding me that life is best enjoyed with a sense of humor, especially when I was knee-deep in numbers.

To my friends, thank you for being there through it all. Your insights, laughter, and occasional reality checks kept me sane (and on track). Whether it was listening to me ramble on about retirement strategies or providing much-needed distractions, you all played a part in making this journey a little lighter.

A heartfelt thanks to my colleagues, past and present, for sharing your knowledge, offering feedback, and helping me see things from new perspectives. You've inspired me to think outside the box and dig deeper into the complexities of retirement planning.

To those who have already navigated the choppy waters of retirement and generously shared your stories—both your triumphs and your challenges—I am deeply grateful. Your willingness to speak candidly about the highs, the lows, and the unexpected twists has been invaluable. Your experiences have shaped this book in more ways than you know.

Lastly, to everyone who has been a part of this journey—whether through advice, support, or simply cheering me on—thank you. This book wouldn't be what it is without you. Here's to the next chapter of life, and may we all find our way to a fulfilling retirement, whatever that looks like!

Forward

Retirement often feels like a distant dream, but with the right plan, it's entirely within your reach. Think of it as building a strong financial foundation that will support you as you leap into the freedom of your golden years. No magic, no luck—just smart strategies, simple math, and a well-executed plan. Whether you're aiming to retire early or at a more traditional age, the goal is the same: to live comfortably and confidently without worrying about money.

Let's be real—early retirement isn't just for the ultra-rich. With a bit of discipline, savvy investing, and avoiding the traps of debt, it's achievable. It's not about scrimping or obsessing over percentages; it's about designing a lifestyle that lets you enjoy life, both now and in retirement. The secret? Stay clear of burdens like mortgages, car loans, and credit card debt. Build a financial plan that can weather any storm, and you'll be able to thrive even during market downturns.

But here's the catch: if you spend your life trying to look successful rather than actually building wealth, you're setting yourself up for a lifetime of work. Chasing the latest gadgets or trying to "keep up with the Joneses" will leave you stuck in the rat race while others are out enjoying their freedom. True success isn't about appearances—it's about securing your financial independence and living life on your terms.

I've seen firsthand how easy it is to fall into financial traps. During the 2008 financial crisis, I watched as people who seemed to have it all lost everything because their wealth was built on credit. Don't let that be your story. Retirement isn't about making it to some magic number; it's about creating a plan that gives you peace of mind, so you can spend your retirement years doing what you love—whether that's traveling the world or mastering your golf swing.

So here's the truth: with the right strategy, early retirement is absolutely possible. It's not just about leaving your job—it's about gaining the freedom to live life on your terms, without the daily grind. Whether you dream of sipping cocktails on a beach or finally tackling that endless reading list, retirement is your chance to live the life you've always imagined.

Plan smart, invest wisely, and most importantly, enjoy the journey—because retirement is just the beginning of the fun!

Chapter 1

What is Early Retirement?

Breaking free from conventional norms, early retirement is about crafting a life that prioritizes personal happiness and fulfillment over traditional career paths. Retiring before the typical retirement age, often between 20 and 50, allows individuals to enjoy greater freedom and live life on their own terms. Hearing personal stories from those who have successfully retired early offers practical advice, inspiration, and a glimpse of what's truly achievable. These stories showcase the diverse ways people reach early retirement, while emphasizing the common themes of determination, financial planning, and lifestyle adjustments needed to accomplish this goal.

"Retirement at sixty-five is ridiculous. When I was sixty-five I still had pimples."
—George Burns

By learning from others' experiences, prospective early retirees can gain insights into the challenges and rewards of this lifestyle. For instance, they can hear about how others managed their finances, what investment strategies they employed, and how they handled unexpected expenses. Personal anecdotes about transitioning from a busy work life to a more relaxed retirement can offer valuable tips on adjusting to the new pace and finding meaningful activities to fill the time.

Experiences from those who have achieved early retirement can highlight the emotional and psychological aspects of early retirement. Retirees can share how they dealt with the identity shift that often comes with leaving a long-term career, the ways they found purpose and fulfillment in new pursuits, and the benefits they've experienced in their relationships and overall well-being. Hearing about real-life experiences can make the abstract idea of early retirement more tangible and achievable, providing a roadmap for those on the same journey. These stories can also serve as a source of motivation and encouragement. Knowing that others have successfully navigated the path to early retirement can boost confidence and resolve. It helps prospective retirees see that while the journey requires careful planning and discipline, it is within reach and can lead to a richly rewarding life.

"Don't act your age in retirement. Act like the inner young person you have always been." —J. A. West

In essence, personal stories enrich the journey toward early retirement by offering insights, practical advice, and emotional support. They underscore the possibilities and freedoms that come with prioritizing personal happiness and fulfillment over conventional career paths. By learning from others who have walked this path, individuals can better prepare themselves to make the most of their time and live life on their own terms. Stories of people who have achieved early retirement offer a compelling glimpse into the varied and inspiring journeys that individuals have embarked on to attain financial independence and a rewarding life well before the traditional retirement age.

"You know you're getting old when you stoop to tie your shoelaces and wonder what else you could do while you're down there." —George Burns

Early retirement sounds like a dream, but it doesn't mean you can completely kick back and forget about generating income or putting in a bit of work. Financial stability still requires some ongoing effort, even if you're not clocking in the traditional 9-to-5 work schedule, whether white or blue-collar. And let's be real—none of those people you see on YouTube are just lounging around; they're making money off of you by getting you to watch their channels, buying their newsletters, and books.

Personal Stories and Testimonials

Here are some inspiring tales of folks who hit the jackpot of early retirement around the age of 55. These legends of leisure had a plan, stuck to it like glue, and ultimately unlocked the dream of ditching the 9-to-5 grind for good. Their stories showcase the magic of disciplined saving (think extreme couponing on steroids), strategic planning (or, as we call it, "How to Retire Without Eating Cat Food"), and smart decision-making (like not buying a yacht just because it was on sale).

"When men reach their sixties and retire, they go to pieces. Women go right on cooking." —Gail Sheehy

Picture this, while their friends are still stuck in traffic on Monday mornings, these early retirees are busy perfecting the art of doing absolutely nothing—or everything they've ever wanted. Whether it's sipping margaritas on a beach, learning to play the ukulele (badly), or finally tackling that 5,000-piece puzzle of the Sistine Chapel, they're living proof that early retirement isn't just a pipe dream—it's a reality for those who plan ahead and avoid the siren call of impulse buys and overpriced avocado toast.

So, if you've ever daydreamed about telling your boss "Take this job and... well, you know the rest," these stories are your blueprint to making that fantasy a reality. Just remember, it's all about playing the long game—and maybe learning how to live with fewer pairs of shoes. Here are some great retirement stories of success people who did it right:

John's Journey to Early Retirement

John spent over 25 years in the tech industry, climbing the corporate ladder and enduring the high-stress environment. By the age of 50, he realized that the relentless pace was taking a toll on his health and happiness. Determined to change his lifestyle, John began saving aggressively, investing wisely, and cutting down on unnecessary expenses. By 55, he had accumulated enough savings to retire early. Now, John spends his days traveling the world with his wife, volunteering at local charities, and indulging in his passion for photography. His early retirement has allowed him to reconnect with his family and rediscover hobbies he had long neglected.

Lisa's Early Retirement Adventure

Lisa worked as a nurse for 30 years, dedicating her life to caring for others. She always dreamed of traveling extensively and writing a book. At 50, after careful financial planning and taking advantage of her employer's retirement benefits, Lisa decided it was time to pursue her dreams. She retired early and embarked on a journey around the world. Lisa now maintains a travel blog, sharing her adventures and inspiring others to explore new cultures. Her early retirement has given her the freedom to live a life filled with excitement and creativity.

Mark and Sarah's Joint Early Retirement

Mark and Sarah, a married couple, both worked in demanding corporate jobs for over two decades. They decided early on that they wanted to retire before 60 to spend more time together and pursue their shared interests. By living frugally, investing in real estate, and maximizing their retirement accounts, they achieved their goal by 55. Now, they run a small organic farm, host workshops on sustainable living, and travel in their RV across the country. Their early retirement has allowed them to live a more meaningful and fulfilling life, focusing on their passions and spending quality time together.

Emma's Financial Independence and Early Retirement

Emma, a software engineer, discovered the concept of financial independence in her early 30s. She was fascinated by the idea of retiring early and began to aggressively save and invest a significant portion of her income. By living below her means and making smart investment choices, Emma was able to retire at 45. She now dedicates her time to mentoring young women in tech, volunteering at animal shelters, and learning new languages. Emma's early retirement has allowed her to give back to the community and pursue lifelong learning, all while enjoying the freedom and flexibility she craved.

Sara's Downsized and Conquered Early Retirement

Sara worked as a financial analyst for over 30 years. She was diligent about saving, maxing out her 401(k), and living below her means. When she turned 50, she decided to downsize from their large suburban home to a smaller, more manageable house in a lower cost-of-living area. This move significantly reduced their expenses, allowing them to save even more. At 55, Sara retired with enough savings and investments to sustain their lifestyle. She now spends time traveling, volunteering, and enjoying hobbies she never had time for before.

James the Teacher Who Invested Wisely

James was a public school teacher for 32 years. Teachers don't always make a lot of money, but James was smart about investing. He started contributing to a Roth IRA and a 403(b) early in his career, taking advantage of the compounding interest over the years. Additionally, he and his wife were frugal, avoiding debt and living modestly. By the time James turned 55, he had enough saved to retire. Now, he spends his days gardening, reading, and spending quality time with his grandchildren.

Maria was an Entrepreneur Who Sold Her Business

Maria ran a small but successful marketing firm for over two decades. She poured her heart and soul into growing the business, but always kept an eye on the future. By her mid-40s, she began planning her exit strategy, ensuring that the business could run without her. At 53, she sold the business for a comfortable sum, which, combined with her savings, allowed her to retire at 55. Maria now enjoys a relaxed lifestyle, traveling extensively and pursuing her passion for painting.

Tom was an Engineer Who Embraced the FIRE Movement

Tom, an engineer, discovered the Financial Independence, Retire Early (FIRE) movement in his 30s. He became obsessed with the idea of retiring early and began saving aggressively, sometimes up to 70% of his income. Tom and his wife lived a very minimalist lifestyle, focusing on experiences rather than material goods. By 55, they had reached their financial independence number and decided to retire. They now live a simple life in a small coastal town, where they enjoy the beach, hiking, and community activities.

Linda was a Nurse Who Made Smart Real Estate Moves

Linda was a nurse who had a knack for real estate. Over the years, she bought and sold several properties, each time upgrading to a better deal. She also invested in rental properties that provided a steady income. By the time she was 55, her real estate investments, combined with her retirement savings, allowed her to retire comfortably. Linda now focuses on her passions: animal rescue and spending time in nature.

These stories show that if you want to retire early in your 40s or 50s, you're going to need somewhere between $600,000 and $1.5 million in savings—basically, the kind of money that makes your piggy bank blush. Of course, this all depends on whether you're planning to live like a hermit in the woods or a celebrity in a mansion. The secret? Save like a squirrel in winter, invest like you're on *Shark Tank*, and live below your means—so your retirement funds don't wave the white flag halfway through!

Reflections on Early Retirement Stories

There's no magic wand when it comes to early retirement—just hard work, careful planning, and smart decisions. These stories highlight the importance of early planning, disciplined saving, smart investing, and sometimes, a bit of luck. Retiring at 55 isn't easy, and it often requires making tough choices along the way. But for those who manage it, the rewards can be a life of freedom, flexibility, and the opportunity to pursue passions that were once put on hold.

In essence, personal stories enrich the journey toward early retirement by offering insights, practical advice, and emotional support. They highlight the possibilities and freedoms that come with prioritizing personal happiness and fulfillment over conventional career paths. By learning from others who have walked this path, individuals can better prepare themselves to make the most of their time and live life on their own terms. John, Lisa, Mark, Sarah, and Emma's stories illustrate that early retirement is not just a financial goal but a gateway to a more fulfilling and purpose-driven life. Next, we'll delve into the benefits of early retirement, dispel common myths, and address potential challenges, such as the loss of identity some may face. With the right planning and strategies, you too can achieve early retirement and create a life centered around your passions and personal fulfillment.

"Aging seems to be the only available way to live a long life."
—*Kitty O'Neill Collins*

But here's the catch: personal stories of early retirement are like cat videos—fun to watch, but they don't give you the full picture. They rarely tell you the real cost of retirement, how much cash they've stashed away, what percentage they're earning on that nest egg, or what they're doing when the market drops faster than your Wi-Fi signal. Most of these tales are just clever ways to rake in revenue, hiding the gritty details to dazzle you with the dream of early retirement. But let's be real: early retirement isn't about kicking back five years before you clock out—unless you hit MegaBucks. It takes serious discipline, starting long before your hair turns gray, or not!

Chapter 2

Why Retire Early?

T here I am, sitting in yet another endless meeting that could've been an email when it hit me: why wait until 65 to enjoy life? Early retirement sounded like the perfect escape plan. No more "clocking in" *per se*, no more dealing with office drama and politics, and no more pretending to be interested in weekly data reporting on the organization's success just to look like I care. It is getting close to the time to trade in my brown leather dress shoes and business casual for flip-flops and board shorts.

"A retired husband is often a wife's full-time job." – Ella Harris

Of course, achieving this dream wouldn't be all sunshine and piña coladas right from the start. I needed to become a financial ninja, mastering the art of saving and budgeting like a pro, understanding withdrawal rates, and managing investments to ensure I wouldn't end up living off ramen noodles and pasta. Not that there's anything wrong with ramen or pasta, but I had bigger culinary ambitions. Before diving into the steps to reach our goals, this book will first cover some of the obstacles we must navigate, what's expected along the way, other popular retirement plans, the advice of financial gurus, actual planning rooted in reality, and how we can create a plan that aligns with one's reality.

Health insurance is another huge puzzle piece for me and my wife when we retire at 55 ½ years of age. Since I wouldn't qualify for Medicare until 65, I had to secure coverage on my own. I decided to ditch corporate America and took a gig at a large state college, where, after 10 years of service, I get the sweet privilege of buying employee health insurance until I'm 65, making the bridge to Medicare as smooth as a freshly paved highway. Unfortunately, early retirement doesn't make you invincible, no matter how good you feel about your decision. But hey, navigating health insurance was just another part of the adventure and I solved it early.

Next up was Social Security. In the United States, you can start claiming benefits as early as 62, but it's described as taking a pie out of the oven too soon – you get less, supposedly. I had to decide if I wanted the smaller slice now or wait for the full pie later. And let's not even talk about accessing retirement accounts early, which felt like dodging boulders in an Indiana Jones movie.

With the newfound free time as a college Professor and Dean, I needed to plan my retirement by reading every book I could, including those from the financial celebrities who make millions off selling their books about retirement to people like me. These books are their way of milking millions from the average person and are their retirement strategy so, read them with skepticism. I also binge-watched YouTube videos by financial heavy hitters on overall retirement and those of the average person living early retirement until my brain turned to mush. My main goal was to ensure that my savings and investments would last through a potentially longer retirement was crucial. Nobody wants to be busking for spare change or stocking shelves at Walmart in their 80s.

"The harder you work, the harder it is to surrender." – Vince Lombardi

Retirement planning offers a smorgasbord of strategies tailored to fit diverse financial goals and lifestyles. Among these, the FIRE (Financial Independence, Retire Early) movement has gained popularity, emphasizing aggressive saving and investment to retire decades earlier than traditional plans. The FIRE movement is all about living like a college student—ramen noodles, hand-me-down clothes, and thrift store furniture included—so

9

you can retire in your 20s, 30s, or 40s. It's a great plan if you enjoy extreme budgeting and minimalist living, but let's be honest, it's a tough road to haul. I mean, who knew retiring early meant mastering the art of DIY retirement savings and becoming a coupon-clipping ninja? In my opinion, this sounds more like a college survival strategy than an adult way of life. We will dive into the FIRE method in detail and many others later in this book.

"Age is an issue of mind over matter. If you don't mind, it doesn't matter."
— Mark Twain

Beyond the ramen-fueled madness of FIRE, there are plenty of other ways to retire without becoming a coupon-clipping ninja. You've got your classic 401(k) and IRA methods, which involve steadily feeding your retirement fund and hoping your employer tosses in a few extra bucks. Some folks prefer the Roth IRA, where you stash away after-tax dollars now for tax-free fun later. Real estate investing is another popular choice, letting you become a landlord and collect rent checks like Monopoly money. Annuities can provide a steady income stream, ensuring you get paid for life, even if it feels like you're signing up for a pension plan from the Middle Ages. Dividend investing focuses on building a portfolio that keeps churning out cash, because who doesn't love getting paid to do nothing? Then there's "semi-retirement," a fancy term for switching to part-time work or freelancing, easing into full retirement like it's a warm bath. Whether you dream of retiring early, mixing work with leisure, or just enjoying a comfy golden age, there's a strategy out there that doesn't involve living like a college student forever.

For me, the 2008 financial market crisis was a wake-up call: retirement was racing towards me faster than a caffeine-fueled intern, and I realized I better start saving properly if I didn't want to end up eating dry cat food. I was only 37 when the crisis hit, which gave me just enough youthful energy to recognize the gaping holes in my saving plan and patch them up for a more comfortable future. Embracing this new reality, I began to maximize my savings, invest wisely, and hunt down every possible income stream like a squirrel on a mission. Living beneath our means became the new household mantra for my wife and me, all in the name of retiring at 55 and enjoying our golden years with some dignity—and maybe even a little spaghetti with sausage.

In the USA, early retirement is like sneaking out of a party before the cake is served – it's typically considered any time before the grand old age of 65. Retiring early in the US somewhere in your 50s with enough money is a pipe dream for most. According to various studies and surveys, only a small percentage of Americans manage to retire comfortably in their 50s. For instance, in 2021 surveys found that about 11% of current retirees had retired before age 60 (Employee Benefit Research Institute, 2021; Fidelity Investments, 2020; Pew Research Center, 2021; Vanguard, 2021). However, having enough money to do so comfortably is another story. Many who retire early either have substantial savings, pensions, or investments according to research (Employee Benefit Research Institute, 2021; Fidelity Investments, 2020; Pew Research Center, 2021; Vanguard, 2021). On the other hand, those following the FIRE movement aim to save 25 to 30 times their current annual expenses, which requires significant financial discipline and income; not an easy task for anyone, especially those with kids.

"You don't stop laughing when you grow old, you grow old when you stop laughing."
– George Bernard Shaw

While exact numbers vary, it's safe to say that successfully retiring in your 50s or younger with enough money is more the exception than the rule. It's like Charlie finding a golden ticket in your chocolate bar – achievable, but rare and requiring some serious planning and luck. This feat involves not just earning a decent income, but also adopting a disciplined saving and investing strategy early on. Many who claim to have achieved early retirement manage to do so involves living extremely frugal by saving as much as 50-70% of their income. This is not realistic for most individuals, couples, and families.

Early retirement requires careful financial planning to account for factors such as healthcare costs, inflation, and unexpected expenses for the next 30 or 40 years. Remember, anything can derail even the best-laid plans, and trying to plan for every scenario is impossible. Most people need to navigate the complex world of investments, balancing risk and return to grow their nest egg sufficiently for 20 or more years unless you are that rare individual who hits the lottery of inheritance, a jackpot, or makes that once-in-a-lifetime lucky stock purchase.

Saving for retirement may be having multiple income streams over and above your current career. This might include real estate investments, dividend-paying stocks, or even side businesses that can provide a steady cash flow during retirement. It's also essential to plan for the long-term, ensuring that your savings will last for several decades, as retiring in your 50s means you could be funding 30 or more years of retirement.

Many Americans are experts at spending more than they earn, treating credit cards like magic wands that conjure up instant gratification. According to data from the U.S. Bureau of Labor Statistics and various financial reports, Americans typically spend about 90% to 95% of their income on essential expenses such as housing, transportation, food, healthcare, and debt payments, with only 5% to 10% allocated to savings and investments (U.S. Bureau of Labor Statistics, 2023). This lifestyle, powered by the siren song of online shopping and "treat yourself" culture, leads to a mountain of debt instead of a pile of savings. It's only when they hit their late 40s or even 50s that the light bulb flickers on, and the panic sets in: "Wait, I need to retire someday?" Cue the frantic scramble to save, with fewer working years left and a retirement fund that looks more like a piggy bank than a treasure chest. It's a bit like trying to cram for a final exam the night before – doable, but far from ideal. So, while we master the art of spending, maybe it's time to throw in a little saving magic too, unless we want to be working forever!

"I found out retirement means playing golf, or I don't know what the hell it means. But to me, retirement means doing what you have fun doing." – Dick Van Dyke

Many Americans struggle to save enough for what is labeled "early retirement" in America for anyone who retires before 65 years of age due to a variety of factors. The high cost of living, including expenses for housing, healthcare, food, education, needs, and most of all, "their wants" makes it difficult to set aside significant savings. Debt from student loans, credit cards, car loans, second mortgages to pay for a dream vacation, and mortgages often take priority over retirement savings. Additionally, a lack of financial education and literacy means many people do not fully understand personal finance (budgeting), investment strategies, or the importance of starting to save early.

Cultural and social factors also play a role. There is a tendency towards immediate gratification and consumption rather than long-term saving, and social pressure to maintain a certain lifestyle can lead to overspending. Income inequality exacerbates the problem, with stagnant wages and low-paying jobs without benefits making it challenging for many to save. Employer-sponsored retirement plans are not universally accessible, and even when they are, participation rates can be low due to a lack of awareness or prioritizing immediate financial needs.

"A thriving new beginning can be and should be a time for amazing engagement, growth, connections, contributions, and amazing possibilities." – Lee M. Brower

Healthcare costs further strain savings, with high medical expenses and insurance premiums draining funds intended for retirement. Economic uncertainty, such as market volatility and job insecurity, can also impact people's ability to save, as they may prioritize immediate financial security over long-term savings. Lifestyle choices, including spending habits and perceptions of retirement as a distant event, lead many to delay saving.

Additionally, longer lifespans mean people need more savings to cover an extended retirement period, which many do not anticipate. Health costs in old age, including long-term care, can further strain retirement savings. Finally, many people underestimate how much they need to save for a comfortable retirement, often failing to account for inflation, which leads to insufficient savings over time.

Job Growth vs. Job Quality: Reality Behind Employment Figures

The U.S. job report frequently emphasizes the number of jobs being created but often overlooks the quality of those jobs. Many new positions are concentrated in low-wage sectors, with a median pay of approximately $36,000 annually. This statistic highlights a noteworthy issue: while the economy may be adding jobs, they are often lower-paying roles that do not necessarily provide sufficient income to keep up with the rising cost of living. This discrepancy raises concerns about the sustainability and economic well-being of the workforce, as many of these jobs may lack the benefits, job security, and wages necessary to support a comfortable standard of living (U.S. Bureau of Labor Statistics, 2023). For a dose of reality, here is a table summarizing the cost of living for someone working in the low-wage sector in Las Vegas, Phoenix, and Los Angeles, compared to the median wage of $36,000 per year:

Expense Category	Las Vegas, NV	Phoenix, AZ	Los Angeles, CA
1 bedroom apartment	$1,200	$1,300	$2,000
Utilities	$250	$200	$250
Transportation -Public	$65	$64	$100
Transportation Car	$500	$450	$600
Groceries	$300	$350	$400
Healthcare (*if they can afford it*)	$300	$300	$350
Estimated Taxes (10%)	$300	$300	$300
Estimated Monthly Expenses	$2,815	$2,964	$3,900
Remaining Income	$85	$36	-$1,000

Despite their best efforts to stretch every dollar, individuals in these low-wage sectors are trapped in a cycle of financial instability, consistently spending more than they earn each month just to cover basic living expenses. This ongoing deficit forces them to rely on credit, deplete any savings they might have, and accumulate mounting debt. Over time, the financial hole deepens, leaving them with no cushion for emergencies and no viable way to dig themselves out. As the pressure of unpaid bills, high-interest loans, and relentless financial obligations continues to grow, they may find themselves facing the harsh reality that their situation is no longer manageable. Eventually, the burden of overwhelming debt and the inability to keep up with payments could lead them to the devastating decision to file for bankruptcy, as it becomes the only way to escape the downward spiral of financial ruin. Just remember when you watch political ads bragging about the high number of jobs one party of the other created that these jobs are low-income and will always be on the treadmill of financial instability; these are not great jobs, they are survival level jobs

In essence, retiring comfortably in your 50s, or any age, is a rare achievement that demands a combination of high income, reprogramming habits, strategic saving, savvy investing, and often a bit of good fortune. Most Americans find it challenging to meet these criteria, so early retirement remains an elusive goal for many. Early retirement is less of a high-stakes gamble and more of a permanent vacation – minus the awkward office dances. Now, as I sip my morning coffee at my desk, I will explain the road one should take, its pitfalls, and the truth about early retirement. One last thing before going on, again, I am not a financial planner, expert, or guru and therefore, you should always consult a licensed financial professional before making any movement or change to your financial situation.

"As your life changes, it takes time to recalibrate, to find your values again. You might also find that retirement is the time when you stretch out and find your potential."
– Sid Miramontes, Retirement: Your New Beginning

All right, here is my political soapboxing, just a friendly reminder: When you watch political ads boasting about how many jobs one party or the other has created, keep in mind that these jobs are often low-income, barely keeping folks on the financial treadmill of survival. These aren't great jobs; they're "just-getting-by" jobs. So, before you get too excited, remember: these politicians are celebrating the creation of jobs that keep people stuck in the hamster wheel of financial instability!

Chapter 3

Retirement Myths and Fantasies

The benefits of early retirement are numerous and can significantly
enhance the quality of life for those who plan strategically. One of
the most compelling advantages is the freedom to do what you want
when you want—without the constraints of a traditional job. Early retirees
have the opportunity to pursue passions, travel extensively, or even start a
new business, all while enjoying the luxury of time that many working
individuals can only dream of. Beyond the thrill of newfound freedom, early
retirement often leads to reduced stress levels and improved overall health.
With the pressures of a demanding job lifted, there's more time to focus on
exercise, healthy eating, and achieving a balanced lifestyle. This newfound
free time also allows for personal development, whether it's learning new
skills, pursuing further education, or simply indulging in hobbies and
interests that were previously sidelined. Moreover, early retirement offers
the priceless gift of spending more quality time with loved ones, fostering
stronger relationships and creating cherished memories.

*"Do not grow old, no matter how long you live. Never cease to stand like curious
children before the great mystery into which we were born."* —*Albert Einstein*

Benefits of Early Retirement

The benefits of early retirement are numerous. One of the most
significant benefits is the freedom to do what you want when you want.

Early retirees can pursue passions, travel extensively, or even start a new business without the constraints of a traditional job. Additionally, early retirement can lead to a reduction in stress levels and an improvement in overall health. Without the pressures of a demanding job, individuals often find more time to exercise, eat healthily, and enjoy a better work-life balance. With more free time, early retirees can focus on personal development, whether it's learning new skills, pursuing further education, or simply enjoying hobbies and interests that were previously sidelined. Furthermore, early retirement provides the opportunity to spend more quality time with loved ones, leading to stronger relationships and cherished memories.

The 4% Rule of Withdrawal (*Bengen rule*)

One of my biggest retirement pet peeves is the 4% rule, a popular guideline for retirement withdrawals. My frustration stems from the fact that it was never intended to be a hard-and-fast rule. Originally introduced by financial planner William Bengen in 1994, the 4% rule was meant to spark discussion and provide a starting point for conversations about sustainable withdrawal rates. However, over time, Certified Financial Planners (CFPs) and other retirement "professionals" have latched onto it and now preach it as the ultimate, one-size-fits-all solution for retirement planning. This oversimplification overlooks the nuanced realities of individual financial situations and changing market conditions, turning what was meant to be a flexible guideline into a rigid doctrine that may not serve everyone's best interests.

"There's never enough time to do all the nothing you want." —Bill Waterson

The 4% rule has an interesting history that traces back to Bengen's 1994 study, where he sought a safe withdrawal rate that retirees could use without running out of money over a 30-year retirement period. Using historical data on stock and bond returns, Bengen examined various withdrawal rates to find the best balance of sustainable income and risk minimization (Bengen, 1994).

Bengen's study analyzed U.S. financial market data from 1926 to 1976, focusing on a balanced portfolio of 50% stocks and 50% bonds. He tested different withdrawal rates to see which would have sustained a retiree's portfolio through the worst market conditions. His research found that a 4% annual withdrawal rate, adjusted for inflation, was the highest rate that would have historically provided a reliable income stream without exhausting the portfolio over 30 years. Additionally, this discussion examined how long $1,000,000 would last a retiree with little growth over the average American retirement span of 25 years, reinforcing the 4% rule as a guideline for ensuring that savings would not be depleted too quickly (Bengen, 1994).

After Bengen published his findings in a paper titled "Determining Withdrawal Rates Using Historical Data," the 4% rule gained significant traction among financial planners and was promoted to retirees. It unfortunately became widely accepted as a simple yet effective guideline for retirement planning. The rule received further validation through the Trinity Study, conducted by three professors from Trinity University in 1998. This study, often cited alongside Bengen's work, confirmed the 4% withdrawal rate's reliability using a similar methodology but with a broader data set and different portfolio compositions (Cooley, Hubbard, & Walz, 1998).

"Retirement, a time to enjoy all the things you never had time to do when you worked."
—Catherine Pulsifer

While the 4% rule remains a cornerstone of retirement planning, it has not been without criticism and debate. Some experts argue that it may be too conservative, while others believe it might be too aggressive, especially in light of changing economic conditions, lower expected future returns, and increased longevity (Fidelity, 2021; CNBC, 2021). In recent years, alternative strategies and adjustments to the 4% rule have been proposed. These include dynamic withdrawal strategies that adjust based on market performance, the "bucket strategy" which separates funds into different categories for short-term and long-term needs, and personalized financial planning that considers individual circumstances and risk tolerances (NerdWallet, 2024; The Balance, 2023).

It is important to understand that the 4% rule is only a guideline and doesn't account for all variables. One major criticism is that it ignores the fact that the stock market has historically grown at an average rate of about 10% per year (Investopedia, 2024). By focusing on the worst-case scenarios and setting a conservative withdrawal rate, the 4% rule may underestimate the potential growth of retirement portfolios. This conservative approach might lead retirees to withdraw less than they could safely afford, thereby reducing their standard of living unnecessarily (Kiplinger, 2023). Additionally, the 4% rule does not take into account the fluctuations of good years and bad years in the market, which can significantly impact retirement savings and withdrawals (CNBC, 2021).

"Retirement is like a long vacation in Las Vegas. The goal is to enjoy it to the fullest, but not so fully that you run out of money." —Jonathan Clements

Moreover, it's important to remember that a Certified Financial Planner (CFP) can only guide you based on the principles and instructions they have been trained to follow. Their guidance, including the 4% rule, is often based on established practices rather than data-driven, personalized, and dynamic strategies that could better accommodate individual circumstances and market variability (NerdWallet, 2024). Its history highlights the importance of data-driven strategies in financial planning and the need for flexibility in adapting to changing economic landscapes (Investopedia, 2024; Kiplinger, 2023). Despite ongoing debates, the 4% rule continues to be a useful starting point for retirees and financial planners, not their only plan.

Dispelling Common Myths and Fears

Dispelling common myths and fears about early retirement can help more people realize that it is not just a dream but an achievable goal. By addressing misconceptions, such as the idea that only the ultra-wealthy can retire early, individuals can see that strategic saving and investment make early retirement possible for many. Furthermore, understanding that early retirees often lead busy, fulfilling lives filled with new interests and pursuits can alleviate fears of boredom and loss of identity.

Myth: Early Retirement Means Boredom

One common myth is that early retirement means boredom without the daily structure of a job. In reality, most early retirees find themselves busier than ever, pursuing new interests, traveling, and spending time with family and friends. Instead of being tied to a desk, they have the freedom to explore passions and hobbies, volunteer for causes they care about, and engage in lifelong learning. Early retirees often discover that they have more time and energy to invest in activities that bring them joy and fulfillment, leading to a richer and more varied life than they had during their working years.

"You don't stop laughing when you grow old, you grow old when you stop laughing."
—*George Bernard Shaw*

A significant fear for many is the risk of outliving their savings. However, with proper financial planning, including creating a budget, managing investments, and planning for healthcare costs, this fear can be mitigated. Early retirees often work with financial advisors to develop a comprehensive plan that accounts for inflation, market fluctuations, and unexpected expenses. They diversify their investment portfolios to balance risk and reward, ensuring that their savings grow steadily over time. Additionally, they plan for healthcare by purchasing insurance or setting aside funds in Health Savings Accounts (HSAs), so they are prepared for medical expenses that arise before they qualify for Medicare.

Fear: Loss of Identity

Finally, some worry that retiring early will lead to a loss of identity since their work defines them. However, many find that early retirement offers the chance to redefine themselves, exploring new roles and identities beyond their careers. They may take on part-time work, start a business, or volunteer in their communities, finding new ways to contribute and stay engaged. Early retirees often report a greater sense of purpose and

20

satisfaction as they pursue interests and goals that align with their values and passions.

For me, I have no fear of losing my identity, rather, being a person with a PhD in environmental geochemist who was once an archaeologist before retooling to geochemistry, worked for large firms like Dames & Moore, Lockheed Martin, IFC Kaiser Engineers, SAIC, started my own professional companies and sold them off, and now the Dean of the School of Science, Engineering, and Mathematics at the College of Southern Nevada, I have no worries about being that "retired guy" playing golf, riding a bike, hanging out with my two kids or grandkids when that comes, or just being that guy who counts nuts and bolts at the local hardware store. Early retirement isn't just about kicking back and sipping margaritas on a beach—though that's a pretty sweet perk. It's about unlocking the ultimate life cheat code: freedom to do what you want, when you want, without the daily grind. Sure, it takes some serious planning, saving like a squirrel before winter, and ignoring those myths that only billionaires can retire early. But once you're there, you can trade in your stress for hobbies, your meetings for meaningful moments, and your work emails for, well, anything else. Early retirement is like leveling up in the game of life—only this time, you're playing by your own rules and having a blast while you're at it. So, if you've ever dreamed of turning your passions into your full-time gig, or just want to finally have time to figure out how to make sourdough bread, early retirement.

Chapter 4

The Illusion of Success

In America, cars, clothing, shoes, purses, sunglasses, and objects often represent a person's identity and status, leading many to invest in such things they can't truly afford. This desire to project an image of success through expensive objects can result in significant financial strain, diverting funds from more critical areas like savings, investments, and retirement planning. It's a costly symbol that ultimately undermines long-term financial health.

Does Your Vehicle Represent My Success

Buying a vehicle offers several advantages. When you buy a car, you own it outright once it's paid off, providing long-term financial benefits as you avoid monthly payments after the loan term. Additionally, purchasing a car builds equity, allowing you to sell the vehicle later and use the proceeds towards another purchase or investment. There are no mileage restrictions, enabling you to drive as much as you need without incurring additional costs, and ownership allows for customization of the vehicle to fit personal preferences and needs (Edmunds, 2023).

"There is a whole new kind of life ahead, full of experiences just waiting to happen. Some call it 'retirement.' I call it bliss." — *Betty Sullivan*

Leasing a vehicle can offer lower monthly payments compared to loan payments, freeing up cash flow for other investments or savings. Leasing often allows you to drive newer models with the latest technology and safety features, and leases typically cover maintenance costs and warranties, reducing out-of-pocket expenses for repairs. Leasing also provides the flexibility to change vehicles every few years without the hassle of selling a used car (CarsDirect, 2023).

When buying a vehicle, it's important to avoid overextending finances by purchasing a more expensive car than necessary, as this can strain your budget and limit your ability to save for retirement. Ignoring depreciation can also be costly, as cars depreciate quickly and buying new means taking a significant hit in value in the first few years. Additionally, not shopping around for financing can lead to higher interest rates and overall costs (Ramsey, 2013).

"Men do not quit playing because they grow old; they grow old because they quit playing." — Oliver Wendell Holmes

With leasing, underestimating mileage can result in costly penalties, and neglecting lease terms can lead to unexpected fees. Continuously leasing without a break means always having a monthly payment, which can add up over time and impact long-term savings (Consumer Reports, 2022).

Cost considerations and their impact on savings are crucial when planning for retirement. The total cost of ownership when buying includes maintenance, insurance, and depreciation, whereas lease costs involve monthly payments, potential mileage penalties, and end-of-lease fees. Leasing might improve short-term cash flow due to lower payments, but long-term costs can be higher without ownership equity. Savings from lower lease payments can be invested, potentially yielding higher returns for retirement. Additionally, owning a car outright after a loan term eliminates a recurring expense, allowing more funds to be directed towards retirement savings (Koblincr, 2017; O'Lcary, 2018).

Long-term financial planning also involves considering asset accumulation, flexibility, and mobility. Buying a car adds to your assets, beneficial for your net worth, while leasing offers flexibility in terms of vehicle use and can be advantageous if your transportation needs change frequently. It's essential to consider how car expenses fit into your overall retirement budget. Lower monthly payments from a lease might help manage cash flow, but the absence of ownership equity could be a drawback (Bogle, 2017; Kiyosaki, 2011).

Ultimately, when deciding between buying and leasing a vehicle with retirement savings in mind, it's crucial to consider both the immediate and long-term financial implications. Buying offers long-term ownership and equity benefits but requires a larger upfront investment, while leasing provides lower monthly payments and flexibility but can result in perpetual expenses without ownership benefits. Carefully assessing your financial situation, driving needs, and retirement goals will help determine the best option for your circumstances.

Financial Mistakes of Vehicle Purchase

When you buy a car, you own it outright once it's paid off, providing long-term financial benefits as you avoid monthly payments after the loan term. Additionally, purchasing a car builds equity, allowing you to sell the vehicle later and use the proceeds towards another purchase or investment. There are no mileage restrictions, enabling you to drive as much as you need without incurring additional costs, and ownership allows for customization of the vehicle to fit personal preferences and needs (Edmunds, 2023).

"Half our life is spent trying to find something to do with the time we have rushed through life trying to save." —*Will Rogers*

Another significant benefit of buying a car is the potential for substantial savings over time. By purchasing a vehicle and keeping it for 10 years or more, you can save a considerable amount of money compared to continually leasing or buying new cars every few years (See table below). Once the car loan is paid off, typically within 3 to 5 years, you no longer have monthly payments. This allows you to redirect the money that would have gone towards car payments into your retirement savings, potentially growing your nest egg significantly (Ramsey, 2013).

When leasing a vehicle, you generally have a lower monthly payment compared to loan payments, freeing up cash flow for other investments or savings (See table below). Leasing often allows you to drive newer models with the latest technology and safety features, and leases typically cover maintenance costs and warranties, reducing out-of-pocket expenses for repairs. Leasing also provides the flexibility to change vehicles every few years without the hassle of selling a used car (CarsDirect, 2023). Leasing perpetually, however, means you will always have a monthly payment. This constant expense can limit your ability to save for retirement effectively. Unlike buying a car, where you eventually eliminate the monthly payment, leasing does not offer an end point to these recurring costs, which can add up significantly over a lifetime (Consumer Reports, 2022).

To illustrate my point, here are two scenarios with people buying versus leasing a car for 20 years. Over a 20-year period, the cost of leasing a car every 3 years versus buying two cars with 60-month loans at 3% interest is significantly different. If you choose to buy two cars with loans ($35,000 purchase price), your total cost over 20 years would be approximately $75,468.50. On the other hand, if you opt to lease a new car that costs $35,000, every 3 years, the total cost would soar to around $210,000. This comparison highlights the substantial financial difference between leasing and buying, with leasing potentially costing nearly three times as much over two decades.

"Congratulations! Today is your day. You're off to great places. You're off and away!"
— Dr. Seuss

I started paying cash for a new car and driving it until it practically begged me to let it retire. When the maintenance costs started looking like I was supporting an aging celebrity's lifestyle, I knew it was time to buy a new one. But here's the kicker—I keep paying that "car payment," except now it goes straight into my savings or retirement accounts. Why? Because I'm not about to let a bank get rich off my hard-earned money. I earned that cash, and I plan to keep every penny growing for my future, not theirs. Why let them sip champagne when I can build my own financial empire?

The True Cost of Car Ownership

Cost considerations and their impact on savings are crucial when planning for retirement. The total cost of ownership when buying includes maintenance, insurance, and depreciation, whereas lease costs involve monthly payments, potential mileage penalties, and end-of-lease fees. Leasing might improve short-term cash flow due to lower payments, but long-term costs can be higher without ownership equity. Savings from lower lease payments can be invested, potentially yielding higher returns for retirement. Additionally, owning a car outright after a loan term eliminates a recurring expense, allowing more funds to be directed towards retirement savings (Kobliner, 2017; O'Leary, 2018).

Long-term financial planning also involves considering asset accumulation, flexibility, and mobility. Buying a car adds to your assets, beneficial for your net worth, while leasing offers flexibility in terms of vehicle use and can be advantageous if your transportation needs change frequently. It's essential to consider how car expenses fit into your overall retirement budget. Lower monthly payments from a lease might help manage cash flow, but the absence of ownership equity could be a drawback (Bogle, 2017; Kiyosaki, 2011).

"Often when you think you're at the end of something, you're at the beginning of something else." — Fred Rogers

When deciding between buying and leasing a vehicle with retirement savings in mind, it's crucial to consider both the immediate and long-term financial implications. Buying offers long-term ownership and equity benefits but requires a larger upfront investment, while leasing provides lower monthly payments and flexibility but can result in perpetual expenses without ownership benefits. Carefully assessing your financial situation, driving needs, and retirement goals will help determine the best option for your circumstances.

Ultimately, I decided to start paying cash for a new car and drive it until it practically begged for mercy. When the repair costs began to rival the GDP of a small country, I'd bite the bullet and buy another one. But here's the twist: instead of giving a bank my hard-earned money in the form of interest, I "pay myself" by funneling those would-be car payments into my savings or retirement accounts. Why let the bank get rich off my hard work? I'd rather keep that sweet, sweet interest for myself, thank you very much. After all, I'm the one who earned it by slogging through endless meetings and surviving office coffee that tastes like burnt rubber. So, why not grow my own money tree and enjoy a prosperous future sipping margarita on a beach, while the bank can go find another sucker to leech off?

Designer Clothes

Today, designer clothes have become a status symbol, with many people purchasing high-end brands to showcase their success and social standing. While sporting the latest fashion trends can certainly boost one's confidence and perceived image, it often comes at a significant financial cost. This expense, much like purchasing an expensive car to impress others, can be detrimental to long-term savings and retirement strategies.

Designer clothes are often associated with wealth and success. People buy them to convey an image of affluence and to fit in with a certain social circle. However, this pursuit of a fashionable façade can lead to overspending. When you regularly buy designer brands, you might be draining your bank account to maintain an image that doesn't reflect your true financial situation. It's an illusion of success that can mask the reality of living paycheck to paycheck or, worse, accumulating debt.

Financial Strain and Opportunity Cost

The financial strain of consistently purchasing expensive clothing can significantly impact your ability to save for the future. Money spent on designer items is money not invested in more substantial financial goals, such as building an emergency fund, paying off debt, or contributing to retirement accounts. The opportunity cost is substantial—every dollar spent on a designer label could have been earning interest in a savings account or growing in an investment portfolio.

27

Impact on Long-Term Savings and Retirement

When prioritizing designer clothes over saving and investing, you risk compromising your long-term financial security. Consistent overspending on luxury items can lead to insufficient retirement savings for the average person, meaning you might have to work longer or live on a tighter budget in your later years. It's important to remember that fashion trends are fleeting, but financial stability is enduring. Investing in your future should take precedence over the temporary satisfaction of owning the latest designer outfit. But hey, if looking like you have $3,000,000 is more important than actually having $3,000,000, go right ahead.

A Balanced Approach

To achieve financial independence and ensure a comfortable retirement, it's crucial to adopt a balanced approach to spending. This doesn't mean you have to completely forgo the pleasure of wearing nice clothes, but it does mean setting priorities. Consider allocating a specific portion of your budget to discretionary spending on fashion while ensuring that the majority of your income is directed toward savings and investments.

"If you look at what you have in life, you'll always have more. If you look at what you don't have in life, you'll never have enough." — Oprah Winfrey

By making mindful choices about where you spend your money, you can still enjoy the occasional luxury item without jeopardizing your financial future. This means setting clear priorities and budgets for discretionary spending while ensuring that a significant portion of your income is allocated to savings and investments. It's about understanding that you don't have to sacrifice style and enjoyment entirely; rather, you need to balance these desires with long-term financial goals. Instead of frequently splurging on high-end items, consider treating yourself occasionally and deliberately, ensuring these purchases are well within your financial means.

Shoes, purses, and other status symbols can significantly derail your retirement plans at any age. These items, often costing hundreds or even thousands of dollars, may provide immediate gratification but can lead to substantial long-term financial consequences. Each purchase represents a missed opportunity to invest in your future. For example, the money spent on a luxury purse could instead be placed in a retirement account, accruing interest and growing over time.

Consistent spending on high-status symbols can result in a lifestyle that is unsustainable in the long run. The financial strain of maintaining such a lifestyle can lead to insufficient retirement savings, forcing you to work longer or compromise on your retirement dreams. Additionally, the habit of spending lavishly can make it challenging to break free from the cycle of consumerism, making it harder to prioritize long-term financial health over short-term desires.

The key is to find a balance that allows you to look good today while also securing a prosperous tomorrow. This involves setting realistic budgets for luxury items and sticking to them. It also means being strategic about your purchases, opting for timeless pieces that offer long-term value rather than succumbing to every fleeting trend. By focusing on quality over quantity and making thoughtful decisions, you can enjoy the benefits of luxury items without compromising your financial future.

"Retirement is a blank sheet of paper. It is a chance to redesign your life into something new and different." — Patrick Foley

The goal is to create a lifestyle that supports both your current desires and your future security. By making mindful choices about where you spend your money, you can enjoy the occasional luxury item while ensuring that the majority of your resources are dedicated to building a stable and prosperous future. This balanced approach helps protect your financial well-being, allowing you to enjoy life now and in retirement without the burden of financial stress.

The Wider Picture of Expenses in America

The average American household allocates a significant portion of its annual income to expenses such as cars, clothing, shoes, purses, and other related items. On average, about 16% of annual income is spent on transportation-related costs, including higher-than-needed car payments, insurance, maintenance, and fuel (U.S. Bureau of Labor Statistics, 2022).

Additionally, approximately 3-4% of income goes toward clothing and other related items, which encompasses designer clothes and luxury items like shoes and purses (U.S. Bureau of Labor Statistics, 2022). In total, Americans spend nearly 19-20% of an American household's annual income dedicated to these expenses. Given that's nearly one-fifth of income spent in areas, it is crucial for individuals aiming for financial stability and retirement savings to manage these costs carefully. Excessive spending on cars and luxury items can detract from the ability to save and invest for the future, emphasizing the need for mindful budgeting and prioritization of long-term financial goals (Kobliner, 2017; O'Leary, 2018).

Ultimately, many Americans appear to be worth millions, donning designer clothes and shoes, driving luxury cars, and living in lavish homes. However, the reality behind this façade is often starkly different. Despite the outward appearance of wealth, many of these individuals live paycheck to paycheck. Their seemingly affluent lifestyles are funded by credit and loans, leaving them with little to no actual savings. The pressure to maintain an image of success leads to excessive spending and financial mismanagement, trapping them in a cycle of debt.

"For many, retirement is a time for personal growth, which becomes the path to greater freedom." — Robert Delamontague

This illusion of prosperity is like a house of cards built on a wobbly table—one unexpected expense, like a surprise medical bill or a leaky roof, could send the whole thing crashing down. These folks might strut around looking like they're worth $10,000,000, but their financial reality is more like Monopoly money—impressive at a glance, but completely useless when the chips are down. It's like driving a luxury car with no gas in the tank; sure, it looks great parked in the driveway, but it's not getting you anywhere. This just goes to show that true financial stability is way more important than putting on a show. After all, you can't pay the bills with appearances, and when the going gets tough, that fancy image won't be much comfort.

"Many people take no care of their money till they come nearly to the end of it, and others do just the same with their time." — Johann Wolfgang von Goethe

I saw this whole charade up close during the financial collapse of 2008. People who looked like they were rolling in dough suddenly found themselves rolling out the welcome mat for bankruptcy. It was like watching a parade of luxury cars all run out of gas at the same time—beautiful on the outside but stuck on the side of the road. These folks strutted around looking like they owned the world, but when the financial storm hit, their so-called wealth evaporated faster than my interest in office small talk. Turns out, their entire empire was built on credit and wishful thinking, and when the bills came due, they didn't have a single cent in savings to bail themselves out. It was a front-row seat to the ultimate reality check: looking rich and being rich are two very different things. If your bank account's empty, that shiny exterior is just a high-gloss illusion—one gust of economic wind, and poof, it's gone!

Chapter 5

The American Culture of Spending

In the heart of American culture lies a vibrant, pervasive ethos: the impulse to spend. It's a deeply ingrained reflex, almost as American as apple pie. When the paycheck arrives and there's a little extra cushion, the first instinct often isn't to stash it away for a rainy day—it's to indulge, to reward ourselves for all that hard work. This spending impulse manifests in a variety of ways, from snapping up the latest fashion accessory that promises to elevate your style game to standing in line for the newest gadget that promises to revolutionize your life (or at least your Instagram feed).

"Dare to live the life you have dreamed for yourself. Go forward and make your dreams come true." — *Ralph Waldo Emerson*

This cultural phenomenon is fueled by a mix of social pressures, clever marketing, and a consumer-driven mindset that equates spending with success; *I call this Vegas Rich.* The idea is simple: if you've got it, flaunt it. And if you don't, well, there's always a credit card to help you pretend you do. The allure of immediate gratification often outweighs the more practical, but less exciting, idea of saving. After all, why save for the future when you can have instant pleasure today?

Let's be honest, there's a certain thrill in spending, in acquiring something new, something shiny, something that promises to make life just a little bit better—even if it's just for a fleeting moment. The culture of spending is wrapped in the notion that possessions can bring happiness, that each new purchase is a step closer to the good life. But beneath this vibrant surface, there's a more complex story—a tale of financial stress, of keeping up appearances, and of a cycle that's hard to break.

So, let's delve into the essence of this cultural phenomenon, where spending has become a way of life, and where the idea of living within one's means is often overshadowed by the desire to live beyond it. In a society where "more" is synonymous with "better," the impulse to spend isn't just about acquiring things—it's about what those things represent: status, success, and, sometimes, a fleeting sense of happiness. One of the most memorable TV commercials where the entire message is spending the savings rather than saving for the future include car insurance,

"Rest is not idleness, and to lie sometimes on the grass under trees on a summer's day, listening to the murmur of the water, or watching the clouds float across the sky, is by no means a waste of time." — *J. Lubbock*

One of the most memorable TV commercials that perfectly encapsulates the "spend your savings" mindset rather than putting it away for the future is the one for car insurance, where a cheerful character celebrates how much they've saved on their premiums. But instead of tucking those savings away into a retirement fund or an emergency savings account, they're shown splurging on extravagant, often absurd, purchases—like a giant inflatable pool flamingo or a backyard full of expensive new gadgets. The entire message is clear: why save for tomorrow when you can have all the fun today? It's a playful yet telling reflection of a culture that often prioritizes immediate gratification over long-term financial security, encouraging us to spend those "extra" dollars the moment we get them. Moreover, marketing leads you to believe that outside optics to the world is more important than the future.

A New Purse, A New Identity

In the world of fashion, a new purse is more than just a utility; it's a statement. For many Americans, especially those influenced by the fast-paced trends of the fashion industry, buying a new purse symbolizes a fresh start, a new identity, and a way to keep up with the ever-changing style landscape. The latest designer bag not only complements an outfit but also signifies status and taste. The joy of purchasing a new purse often outweighs the practicality of saving the money, as the immediate gratification and social approval provide a significant emotional boost.

Toys, Gadgets, and the Pursuit of Happiness

Whether it's the latest smartphone, a high-tech gadget, or even a collectible action figure, the allure of new toys is undeniable. For adults and children alike, these toys represent more than just objects—they are symbols of progress, innovation, and sometimes nostalgia. The act of buying these items can evoke a sense of excitement and fulfillment, making it a popular choice for those with extra cash. In American culture, where technological advancements and consumerism are deeply intertwined, the impulse to buy the latest toy often trumps the idea of putting money into a savings account.

The Spend-First Mentality

The broader narrative in American society often revolves around the notion of living in the moment. The philosophy of "you only live once" (YOLO) encourages people to seize the day and enjoy their earnings rather than hoard them for an uncertain future. This mentality is further fueled by advertising campaigns that emphasize the joy and satisfaction derived from immediate consumption. The result is a culture where spending money on discretionary items becomes a norm, and saving is often an afterthought.

The Role of Advertising and Social Media

Marketing plays a crucial role in perpetuating the spend-first culture. Companies invest heavily in creating ads that tap into consumers' emotions, promising happiness, success, and social acceptance through their products. Social media platforms amplify this effect by showcasing influencers and peers enjoying their latest purchases, creating a sense of urgency and FOMO (fear of missing out). The desire to keep up with trends and appear affluent drives many Americans to prioritize spending over saving.

Commercials: Promoting Spending Over Saving

A notable aspect of this culture is how commercials often prioritize promoting spending rather than saving, particularly for long-term goals like retirement. Advertisements bombard consumers with messages that highlight the immediate benefits of spending money on luxury items, entertainment, and the latest trends. Rarely do they emphasize the importance of saving for retirement or building a financial safety net. This pervasive messaging reinforces the idea that spending brings happiness and fulfillment, whereas saving is seen as a less attractive, albeit necessary, activity.

The Financial Implications

While the culture of spending can indeed provide immediate pleasure, it often comes with significant long-term financial consequences. The thrill of acquiring the latest trends, gadgets, or luxury items can be intoxicating, creating a temporary sense of satisfaction and status. However, this pursuit of instant gratification can quickly spiral into a cycle of debt, especially when purchases are made on credit without careful consideration of future repercussions. Many Americans find themselves trapped in this cycle, with credit card bills steadily piling up, leading to financial stress and anxiety. Instead of building wealth, the focus shifts to managing debt, making it increasingly difficult to break free from the financial strain that accompanies this lifestyle.

"Retirement is a time for personal growth, which becomes the path to greater personal freedom."– Mark Evan Chimsky

Moreover, the lack of robust savings habit exacerbates this issue, leaving individuals particularly vulnerable to financial emergencies. Without a cushion to fall back on, an unexpected expense—whether it's a medical emergency, car repair, or job loss—can quickly derail one's financial stability. This lack of preparedness also limits the ability to invest in the future, such as contributing to retirement accounts or taking advantage of investment opportunities that could lead to long-term financial growth. The result is a precarious financial situation where the pursuit of short-term pleasure comes at the expense of long-term security. Building a habit of saving and investing, even in small amounts, is essential to creating a stable financial foundation that not only supports immediate needs but also secures a more prosperous future.

Finding Balance

Understanding this cultural inclination towards spending is crucial for developing a healthier, more balanced approach to personal finance. In a world where instant gratification and the allure of shiny new things are constantly tugging at our wallets, it's easy to get caught up in the thrill of spending. After all, there's nothing wrong with enjoying the fruits of your labor—life is meant to be lived, and splurging on the occasional treat or experience can bring genuine joy and satisfaction.

However, the challenge lies in not letting this impulse overshadow the importance of saving and investing for the future. While it feels great to indulge in the present, it's equally important to cultivate the habit of setting aside a portion of your income for long-term goals. Whether it's building an emergency fund, investing in a retirement account, or saving for a significant future purchase, these disciplined actions provide the financial security and peace of mind that allow you to truly enjoy life without the constant stress of financial uncertainty.

"Retirement is a time for personal growth, which becomes the path to greater personal freedom."– Mark Evan Chimsky

Striking a balance between spending on the things that bring you happiness and setting aside funds for future needs is key to achieving long-term financial well-being. It's about making mindful choices—recognizing when a purchase will genuinely enhance your life versus when it's just a fleeting desire driven by external pressures. By prioritizing both present enjoyment and future security, you can create a financial strategy that not only supports your lifestyle today but also ensures that you're prepared for whatever the future may hold.

This balanced approach empowers you to enjoy the best of both worlds: the freedom to live well now and the confidence that comes with knowing you're building a solid financial foundation for the years ahead. Ultimately, it's not about depriving yourself but about making smart decisions that allow you to savor life's pleasures while securing a comfortable and stable future.

In conclusion, the American culture of spending is a multifaceted phenomenon driven by the desire for instant gratification, social validation, and the influence of marketing and media. Recognizing these drivers can help individuals make more informed decisions about their finances, ensuring that their spending habits align with their long-term goals and aspirations. The sneaky power of marketing and our culture's obsession with looking good have tricked a lot of us into prioritizing what others think over what's actually in our bank accounts. It's like we've all been convinced that impressing the neighbors is more important than making sure we don't end up living in their basement someday. This obsession with looking like a million bucks—fueled by the need for status, acceptance, and the occasional "Wow, you're doing so well!"— often blinds us to the fact that a solid financial foundation is way more valuable than the latest designer handbag or shiny new gadget.

"The question isn't at what age I want to retire, it's at what income." —George Foreman

The lure of instant gratification and the pressure to keep up appearances can trap us in a spending cycle that sacrifices long-term stability for fleeting moments of "I've still got it!" And before you know it, you're investing more in your image than in your future, all while forgetting that true success isn't about what's on display—it's about having the freedom to live life on your own terms without worrying about whether your credit card bill is about to burst into flames.

Here's the deal: while it's oh-so-tempting to splurge on the latest must-have items and live for today, the real win comes from planning wisely for tomorrow. After all, those flashy purchases might make you look good now, but it's your financial independence that'll have you really living the good life—long after the shine has worn off those designer shoes.

Chapter 6

The United States of Debt

A mericans, on average, live far beyond their means, often spending much more than they earn or should. This trend is fueled by a combination of consumer culture and the pressure to maintain a certain lifestyle, leading to a cycle of accumulating debt. Financial expert Dave Ramsey notes that many people allocate between 20% and 30% of their post-tax income just to service their debts, which include car loans, student loans, personal loans, and credit card balances—excluding their mortgage or rent payments. This debt is often a result of individuals striving to "keep up with the Joneses," purchasing expensive cars, homes, and luxury items to project an image of wealth to friends and family. As a result, many Americans find themselves with a high debt-to-income ratio, where a substantial portion of their income is consumed by interest payments and principal repayments, leaving little room for savings or financial security.

"Retirement, a time to do what you want to do, when you want to do it, where you want to do it and how you want to do it," – Catherine Pulsifer

For instance, the average American household carries about $15,000 in credit card debt, which translates into significant monthly payments that can severely restrict disposable income. Additionally, many households finance their day-to-day lifestyle with loans, effectively living on borrowed money rather than their actual earnings. This behavior not only limits their ability to save for retirement but also creates ongoing financial stress and instability. The average American household's debt burden is staggering, enough to make any wallet weep and a calculator run out of digits. Mortgage debt is the largest chunk, with the median mortgage debt sitting at an eye-popping $215,655—an amount that could almost buy a small island, if such were available for purchase. Credit card debt comes next, with households carrying around $15,000 in balances, often spent on things that seemed like a good idea at the time, like that "essential" chocolate fountain (Ramsey Solutions, 2024). Auto loans add another $28,000 to the debt pile, driven by the allure of that shiny new car smell. And let's not forget student loans, where the average borrower owes about $37,000—clearly, the cost of knowledge doesn't come cheap (Politico, 2024). When you add it all up, the average household is saddled with roughly $101,915 in total debt, which is about as comfortable as sleeping on a porcupine pillow (Debt.org, 2024). Managing this mountain of debt is crucial for financial stability, but at least one's credit score gets a thorough workout in the process!

American Spending Habits

To understand how an American earning $100,000 per year typically spends their income, we can look at some general spending categories, although these can vary depending on factors like location, lifestyle, and financial obligations. On average, taxes (including federal, state, Social Security, and Medicare) consume about 25-30% of the income, equating to $25,000 to $30,000 annually (U.S. Bureau of Labor Statistics, 2024). Housing costs, which often represent the largest single expense, typically take up 25-35%, or $25,000 to $35,000, and include rent or mortgage payments, utilities, property taxes, and maintenance (U.S. Bureau of Labor Statistics, 2024). Transportation expenses, including car payments, insurance, gas, and public transport, usually account for 10-15%, or $10,000 to $15,000 (U.S. Bureau of Labor Statistics, 2024). Food expenses, covering both groceries and dining out, also make up about 10-15% of the budget (U.S. Bureau of Labor Statistics, 2024). Healthcare costs, including insurance premiums and out-of-pocket expenses, generally range from 5-10%, or $5,000 to $10,000 (U.S. Bureau of Labor Statistics, 2024). Savings and investments, such as retirement accounts and emergency funds, typically represent 10-15% of income (MyMoney.gov, 2024). Debt payments, like those for credit cards or student loans, often account for 5-10% of the budget (U.S. Bureau of Labor Statistics, 2024). Discretionary spending on non-essentials like entertainment, travel, and hobbies can take up 10-20%, or $10,000 to $20,000, while miscellaneous expenses like clothing, gifts, and charity usually range from 5-10% (MyMoney.gov, 2024).

In summary, essential expenses like housing, transportation, food, healthcare, and debt payments can gobble up 55-75% of your income, while discretionary spending might devour another 15-30%, leaving savings to nibble on the last 5 to 10%. For instance, if you're making $100,000 a year, you could find yourself spending 60% on essentials ($60,000), 20% on wants ($20,000), and squeezing out a modest 5 to 10% for savings ($5,000 - 10,000), all while Uncle Sam takes his 25% cut ($25,000). These figures paint a picture of how your hard-earned cash might be sliced and diced, though everyone's situation is a little different. But with needs, wants, healthcare, and taxes chewing up so much of your paycheck, there's barely enough left for a rainy-day fund—let alone that dream yacht!

"For retirement brings repose, and repose allows a kindly judgment of all things."
— John Sharp Williams

Stop spending money just to look rich and start saving to become rich. The truly wealthy aren't the ones flaunting the latest gadgets or luxury items—they're the ones who can retire comfortably and enjoy life after working hard for 30 or 40 years. Real wealth is measured by the freedom to live on your own terms, not by draining your money into creditors' pockets or by keeping up with the Joneses. Focus on building a solid retirement fund instead of splurging on things that lose value the moment you buy them.

My Favorite, Student Loan Debt

A significant portion of this debt crisis is driven by student loans. Many Americans are burdened with substantial student loan debt due to the widespread belief that attending a "good university" is essential for success. However, the notion of what makes a university "good" often centers on vague and misleading ideas like reputation and prestige, rather than the actual quality of education. In reality, any accredited institution can provide a solid education, and the value of a bachelor's degree remains largely consistent regardless of the school. This misconception has contributed significantly to the student debt crisis, particularly for those attending expensive private universities or out-of-state public institutions. For instance, students attending universities as non-residents often graduate with debt ranging from $50,000 to over $250,000, while those at "prestigious" private universities may face even higher levels of debt, sometimes exceeding $250,000. Folks, this is just for a bachelor's degree—those who pursue master's or doctoral degrees often incur even more debt.

"The best university is the one that lets you graduate with the least debt"

To put this into perspective, consider the estimated cost for non-resident students to attend the University of California (UC) in the 2025-26 academic year—tuition with room and board alone is projected to approach $80,000 per year. It's easy to see how quickly debt can accumulate under such circumstances. I know of a young man, for instance, who attended UC Irvine for his bachelor's degree and graduated with a staggering $240,000 in student loan debt. He could have attended a local major university in his home state for the same degree and incurred less than $50,000 in debt. Does that sound like good debt? Not even close!

"Working people have a lot of bad habits, but the worst of these is work."
— Clarence Darrow

These trends are like a financial horror show, where non-resident students and those at private institutions walk away with debt levels that could rival a small mortgage. Meanwhile, their in-state and public university buddies are cruising along with way less financial baggage. This massive mountain of debt doesn't just chain you to your student loan servicer; it also throws a big, wet blanket on your future financial freedom. I have always said that "Only fools put their kids in universities that will ultimately crush them financially"—it's like signing them up for a lifetime of paying off someone else's mansion instead of building their own. With current student loan debt in the U.S. reaching a staggering $1.7 trillion as of August 2024, it's as if we're saying, "Hey, let's pay a fortune for a diploma that might not even cover the return on investment!" Yeah, not the best deal.

For individuals with advanced degrees, such as a master's, PhD (Doctor of Philosophy), or even professional level degrees like an EdD (Doctor of Education), DDS (Doctor of Dental Surgery), DO (Doctor of Osteopathic Medicine), JD (Juris Doctor), or MD (Doctor of Medicine), the median student loan payment is generally higher than the overall median, typically ranging from $750 to $2,500 per month in addition to their debt from their undergraduate degree (U.S. Department of Education, 2023). However, for those with significant loan balances—common among holders of a PhD and professional degrees—monthly payments can be much higher, sometimes exceeding $1,000 per month, particularly on a standard 10-year repayment plan (Federal Reserve, 2023). These higher payments reflect the larger loan amounts often associated with such degrees. It's important to note that these figures can vary depending on the repayment plan selected, such as income-driven repayment plans, which may result in lower monthly payments based on the borrower's income and other individual factors.

"For many, retirement is a time for personal growth, which becomes the path to greater freedom." – Robert Delamontague

As of recent data, the student loan default rate in the United States is approximately 15%, meaning that about 15% of borrowers have not made a payment on their federal student loans for at least 270 days, the threshold for a loan to be considered in default (U.S. Department of Education, 2023). This default rate can vary depending on factors such as the type of institution attended (e.g., public vs. private, for-profit vs. non-profit) and prevailing economic conditions. Additionally, changes in federal policies and the availability of different repayment options can also influence the default rate over time (Federal Reserve, 2023).

In conclusion, the American obsession with living beyond one's means is a ticking financial time bomb. The relentless pursuit of status symbols like luxury cars, oversized homes, and the latest gadgets drives many into a cycle of debt that eats away at their income, leaving little room for savings or long-term financial security. This trend is exacerbated by the societal pressure to keep up with the Joneses, leading to decisions that prioritize appearances over financial stability. The staggering debt levels many Americans face—whether from mortgages, credit cards, auto loans, or student loans—are a clear indicator of the precariousness of this lifestyle.

True wealth isn't about looking rich today; it's about being financially free tomorrow. The path to real financial security lies in prudent spending, diligent saving, and a long-term focus on retirement. By choosing to save and invest wisely rather than spending to impress others, individuals can break free from the debt cycle and secure a future where they can enjoy the fruits of their labor without the burden of financial stress. Remember, the richest person isn't the one with the flashiest lifestyle; it's the one who can retire with peace of mind, knowing they've built a solid foundation for their future.

"Retire from work, but not from life." – M.K. Soni

The true mark of wealth isn't in the car you drive, the university you attend, or the size of the house you own; it's in the financial freedom to live life on your terms. By resisting the urge to keep up with the Joneses and instead focusing on building a solid financial foundation, you can create a future where stress and debt aren't the main characters in your life story. So, the next time you're tempted by that shiny new toy or the latest must-have gadget, remember real wealth isn't about impressing others today—it's about securing your peace of mind for tomorrow.

Chapter 7

Spending that Sabotages Retirement

Many Americans waste money on everyday expenses that could be invested in their retirement. For instance, dining out frequently or ordering takeout can significantly drain finances, as the cost of eating out is much higher than cooking at home (National Restaurant Association, 2021). Subscription services, such as streaming platforms and gym memberships, are often underutilized, and canceling unnecessary subscriptions can free up funds for retirement investments (Statista, 2022). Daily trips to coffee shops, costing about $5 each time, can amount to over $1,800 annually, which could be saved by brewing coffee at home (Investopedia, 2023). Impulse purchases, whether online or in stores, lead to unnecessary expenditures, and creating a budget can help prevent these spontaneous buys (The Balance, 2023).

High-Interest Rate Wasting

Additionally, carrying a balance on credit cards and paying high-interest rates is a common financial mistake. Paying off credit card debt quickly can save money on interest, which can then be invested for retirement (Consumer Financial Protection Bureau, 2023). Spending excessively on luxury vehicles, which depreciate quickly, can be a significant financial drain. Opting for a more affordable, reliable car can reduce monthly payments and maintenance costs, freeing up funds for retirement savings (Edmunds, 2023). Purchasing high-end fashion items to keep up with trends can be costly, and focusing on quality over quantity can save a lot of money (Money Crashers, 2023). Regularly upgrading to the latest smartphones, electronics, or home appliances can be an unnecessary expense, and using items until they no longer function properly can help save money for more important financial goals (CNET, 2023).

The Gym Rate You're Not

This is my ultimate favorite wasting of American's money, paying for a gym membership you never use is like signing up for a marathon and then deciding your couch is a better training ground. Instead, try affordable fitness options like outdoor activities or home workouts that won't just save you money but might get you moving (NerdWallet, 2023). Overpaying for insurance policies without shopping around is like buying the first car you see at the dealership—blindfolded. Compare plans and negotiate for better rates to save those extra dollars for your golden years (Forbes Advisor, 2023). Regularly spending money on lottery tickets and gambling is basically donating to the "I Hope I Get Lucky" fund with terrible odds. Steer clear of these habits to keep your wallet happy and healthy (CNBC, 2023).

Household Operations and Random ATM Fees

High utility bills can suck your finances dry. Implementing energy-saving measures is like putting your bills on a diet—they'll slim down, and so will your expenses (Energy.gov, 2023). Lastly, paying unnecessary bank fees, such as overdraft charges and ATM fees, is like throwing a party for your bank every month. Choose a bank with lower fees and manage your accounts wisely to keep more of your hard-earned cash where it belongs—in your pocket (Bankrate, 2023).

"It is better to have a permanent income than to be fascinating." — *Oscar Wilde*

Finally, by identifying and eliminating these common areas of wasteful spending, Americans can redirect significant amounts of money into their retirement savings. It's like finding cash between your couch cushions—except this time, it's enough to buy a small island. Making small changes in daily habits and spending patterns can accumulate substantial savings over time, transforming your future from a financial anxiety fest into a comfortable retirement oasis.

Money wasted on various expenses as a percentage of their annual income, assuming an average annual income of $50,000 is presented in the table below:

Category	Annual Cost (%)	Annual Cost
Dining Out/Takeout	6	$3,000
Subscription Services	1	$500
Daily Coffee Trips	3.6	$1,800
Impulse Purchases	4	$2,072
Credit Card Interest	2	$1,036
High-End Fashion	3	$1,500
Gym Memberships	1	$500
Overpaid Insurance	1.2	$600
High Utility Bills	2.4	$1,200
Bank Fees	0.4	$200

When it comes to everyday spending, imagine swapping out that daily $5 coffee for a home-brewed cup of joe. In no time, you'll have enough saved to buy your own coffee plantation. Consider cutting out those subscription services you forgot you even had—say goodbye to the $10-a-month pet yoga channel and hello to a heftier retirement fund. And don't forget the miracle of energy-saving measures; it's like your utility bills went on a crash diet and actually stuck to it. By making these tweaks, you're not just saving pennies; you're setting up a retirement where you're the one throwing the parties, not your bank. So, take a look at your spending habits, trim the fat, and watch your savings grow. Your future self, lounging on a beach with a piña colada in hand, will thank you.

"It's not how much money you make, but how much money you keep, how hard it works for you, and how many generations you keep it for." — *Robert Kiyosaki*

By trimming the fat from your budget, you're not just pinching pennies; you're laying the groundwork for a retirement where you're the one enjoying life, not stressing over finances. Picture yourself in the future, lounging on a beach with a piña colada in hand, knowing that your smart financial choices today made it all possible. So, start cutting out those unnecessary expenses, watch your savings grow, and look forward to a future where you're the one throwing the parties, not your bank. Your future self will be raising a glass in gratitude.

Finally, building strong habits around saving now and practicing financial constraint is key to securing a successful retirement. By consistently saving early and avoiding impulsive spending, individuals create a solid foundation for financial independence. Small, disciplined efforts in budgeting and setting aside funds compound over time, ensuring greater financial security during retirement. These habits help individuals resist the pressures of consumer culture and avoid debt, ultimately enabling them to enjoy a more comfortable and worry-free retirement in the future.

Chapter 8

Counter to Financial Gurus

Many financial experts love to tell you that you'll need to replace a whopping 80-95% of your pre-retirement income to maintain your standard of living. But let's be real—those experts might just be using the same math that says you can't have dessert before dinner. When you actually take a peek at what you're living on versus what you're earning while working, the real figure is closer to 60-63% of your salary. Why the big difference? Well, once you retire, you can say goodbye to expenses like retirement account contributions, Social Security contributions, Medicare taxes contributions, and all those work-related costs like commuting, dry-cleaning your office/work clothes, and pretending to enjoy office birthday parties.

So, the idea that you'd need 80%, 90%, or even 95% of your pre-retirement income in retirement doesn't quite add up—unless, of course, you plan on using that extra cash to start a luxury llama farm. Plus, you'll likely be paying lower taxes in retirement, and with no more work-related expenses, you might find yourself with more money in your pocket than when you were grinding away at the office. Ideally, by the time you're ready to retire, you've kicked all those pesky debts to the curb—credit card balances, student loans (because who wants to be paying off college when you're 70?), car loans, and a high mortgage.

With some smart planning, you'll find that retirement is a lot more affordable than you might've thought. By cutting back on unnecessary expenses, tweaking your saving strategies, and not buying into those sky-high benchmarks, you can kick back, relax, and enjoy your golden years without wondering if you should be clipping coupons for cat food.

Financial Guru Rhetoric

Financial gurus like Susie Orman, Dave Ramsey, Carl Icahn, and others have a knack for making wallets quiver. Susie Orman has been quoted that you need at least $5,000,000 to retire comfortably (Financial Samurai, 2023), claiming this massive stash is essential to cover daily living expenses, healthcare costs, inflation, and those pesky financial emergencies. However, let's be real—this simply isn't true for everyone. While her advice aims to turn you into a supersaver, it can also make you feel like you need to strike gold just to take a nap. Critics argue that her sky-high figures scare people away from the idea of early retirement or have them clutching their piggy banks in fear. The truth is, retirement planning isn't a one-size-fits-all scenario; it's more like a choose-your-own-adventure book, where the amount you need depends on your circumstances, lifestyle, and goals. So, before you start panicking and buying lottery tickets, remember that your retirement dreams might not require a billionaire's bank account—just some smart planning and a good sense of humor.

"Retirement: That's when you return from work one day and say, "Hi, Honey, I'm home — forever." – Gene Perret

Another misconception is that early retirement is only achievable for the ultra-wealthy. While it does require careful financial planning and discipline, many regular people achieve early retirement through strategic saving, investing, and living below their means. They make conscious choices to prioritize long-term financial security over short-term gratification, such as opting for a modest lifestyle, reducing debt, and investing in assets that generate passive income. By taking advantage of tax-advantaged retirement accounts, employer matches, and the power of compound interest, even those with average incomes can build a nest egg that supports early retirement. The key is to start planning early, stay committed to financial goals, not give in to your spending urges for all your wants, and make informed decisions about spending and saving.

Keeping up with the Joneses phenomenon

Americans are significantly impacted by the phenomenon of "keeping up with the Joneses." This is one thing I agree with when it comes to their salesman and saleswoman style agenda. This mindset is deeply ingrained in American culture, where individuals strive to match or surpass the lifestyle and social status of their neighbors, friends, family, and peers. This drive often leads to conspicuous consumption and financial overextension, as people purchase expensive items such as homes, cars, and other luxury goods to project an image of wealth and success. Social media and reality TV have greatly amplified the visibility of affluent lifestyles, making it easier for people to compare their own lives with those of others, creating pressure to emulate these lifestyles (Kasser, 2002). The American economy heavily promotes consumerism, with marketing and advertising encouraging the purchase of the latest products, leading individuals to equate material possessions with happiness and success (Schor, 1998).

Many Americans finance their lifestyles through credit, resulting in significant debt. As Dave Ramsey explains, American households often allocate up to 20% of their income toward debt payments, which can include car loans, student loans, credit cards, unsecured signature loans, and of course, rent and mortgage payments (Federal Reserve, 2023). This debt is often incurred to maintain appearances and keep up with social expectations. The desire to keep up with others can lead to stress and dissatisfaction, as individuals who base their self-worth on financial success and material possessions are more likely to experience lower well-being and higher levels of anxiety (Dittmar, 2008).

"Often when you think you're at the end of something, you're at the beginning of something else." – Fred Rogers

The pursuit of a certain lifestyle can lead to high levels of personal debt, with the average American household debt, including significant amounts from mortgages, auto loans, and credit cards, often exceeding $101,915 in total (LendingTree, 2024). As people spend more to maintain their lifestyle, they often save less, impacting their long-term financial security and their ability to handle emergencies and save for retirement. To mitigate this phenomenon, there is a growing movement toward minimalism and financial independence. Emphasizing financial literacy, budgeting, and the value of experiences over material goods can help individuals make more informed financial decisions and reduce the pressure to keep up with the Joneses. This cultural phenomenon underscores the need for greater financial education and a shift towards valuing financial stability over superficial appearances.

In conclusion, while financial experts might have you believe that you need to replace 75-80% of your pre-retirement income to keep living the good life, the reality is more like a well-budgeted grocery trip—totally manageable and possibly with some coupons. Once you ditch the expenses like retirement contributions, Social Security, Medicare taxes, and the daily grind of work-related costs, you can probably cruise through retirement on a cool 60-63% of your former paycheck. The real secret to retiring in style isn't about obsessing over percentages; it's about smart planning, living within your means, and knowing what works for your bank account. With a solid strategy and a laser focus on kicking debt to the curb, most folks can kick back in retirement without needing to hit those sky-high income replacement goals that financial gurus love to shout about. Remember, retirement planning isn't a one-size-fits-all marathon; it's more like a leisurely stroll that should prioritize your peace of mind over keeping up with the Joneses or chasing pie-in-the-sky savings targets. Hence, relax, plan smart, and enjoy your golden years—because the best kind of retirement is the one that lets you sleep easy at night, not the one that makes you lose sleep over percentages.

Chapter 9

Setting Early Retirement Goals

S etting early retirement goals is like mapping out your dream vacation: the sooner you plan, the sooner you get to enjoy the destination. By defining clear financial targets now and sticking to a consistent saving strategy, you can pave the way to a life of freedom and adventure well before the traditional retirement age. It's not just about quitting work early; it's about having the financial flexibility to live life on your own terms.

Save Aggressively

Achieving early retirement is a dream for many, and while it requires careful planning and discipline, it is entirely possible with the right strategies. One of the most effective approaches is to save aggressively. Experts recommend aiming to save at least 50% of your income, as the higher your savings rate, the sooner you can retire (Kobliner, 2017). Automating savings by setting up automatic transfers to retirement accounts ensures consistent saving without the temptation to spend (O'Leary, 2018).

Investing wisely is another crucial strategy. Diversifying investments in the stock market through index funds or ETFs that track the overall market has historically provided solid returns over the long term (Bogle, 2017). Additionally, investing in real estate, such as rental properties or Real Estate Investment Trusts (REITs), can generate passive income and provide a steady cash flow (Kiyosaki, 2011).

Maximize your savings but not if it hurts your quality of Life

Maximizing contributions to tax-advantaged retirement accounts, such as 401(k)s and IRAs, is essential. Taking full advantage of employer matching contributions in a 401(k) and investing in a Roth IRA for tax-free growth and withdrawals in retirement can significantly boost your retirement savings (IRS, 2023). Reducing expenses by adopting a frugal lifestyle and cutting unnecessary costs can also increase your savings rate and reduce the amount you need for retirement (Roth, 2019).

Early multiple income streams

Generating multiple income streams is a powerful way to accelerate your path to early retirement. Starting a side business or freelancing can provide additional income, while building passive income streams through investments, such as dividends, interest, and royalties, can offer financial stability (Sabin, 2020). Tax optimization strategies, like tax-loss harvesting to offset gains and strategic withdrawals during lower-income years, can minimize your tax liability (Piketty, 2014).

"Stay young at heart, kind in spirit, and enjoy retirement living." —*Danielle Duckery*

Hey, I have a PhD in environment soil chemistry, I work in the science service sector, and I have no issues earning money from income streams that might not typically be associated with my financial or educational status. To be quite honest, I don't care what others think because I'll be sipping piña coladas long before my colleagues can retire.

There is no "Good Debt"

Paying off debt, especially high-interest debt like credit cards, car loans, and personal loans is critical to reducing financial burdens (Ramsey, 2013). Consider paying off your mortgage early to lower monthly expenses and free up more money for savings. Maintaining an emergency fund with 6-12 months of living expenses is also essential to cover unexpected costs without derailing your savings plan (Orman, 2016).

Heck, for me, paying off our mortgage is like hitting the jackpot—I'm saving almost $1,500 a month in interest and principal payments that I was throwing away before! It's like getting a raise without lifting a finger. And let's be real, in today's world, carrying a mortgage into retirement is like dragging a ball and chain around. What used to be considered "good debt" is now just a heavy anchor when you're trying to sail smoothly into your golden years. Better to cut that chain loose and enjoy the financial freedom!

Why live in a huge house

Many of my colleagues spend lavishly on huge homes or decorate their homes to look like they are on an episode of the "Rich and Famous" to impress others. I realized that a house doesn't represent who I am or your success. The cost of maintaining a large, impressive home can be a financial drain, consuming funds that could otherwise be invested in growth. Downsizing to a smaller home or moving to a lower-cost-of-living area can further reduce expenses and free up more money for savings (Vanderkam, 2015). By living below my means, I can focus on what truly matters to me rather than seeking validation through material possessions.

Health Care Planning

Planning for healthcare costs is crucial for early retirees. Unlike those who retire at the traditional age and can rely on Medicare, early retirees need to bridge the gap until they become eligible for these benefits (Hoffman, 2022). This makes it essential to thoroughly research health insurance options, such as the Health Insurance Marketplace, COBRA, or even coverage through a spouse's plan (Ferri, 2016). These options can help ensure that you maintain adequate healthcare coverage without draining your retirement savings.

"Count your age by friends, not years." —*John Lennon*

But healthcare isn't the only thing you need to keep an eye on. Regular financial reviews and adjustments to your retirement plan are key to staying on track. This includes periodically rebalancing your investment portfolio to ensure it aligns with your risk tolerance and retirement timeline. As your circumstances and goals evolve, so too should your retirement strategy. For instance, you might find that your priorities shift, requiring you to update your retirement goals or adjust your spending habits. By staying proactive and flexible, you can navigate the complexities of early retirement with confidence, ensuring that your nest egg remains robust enough to support the lifestyle you've worked so hard to achieve.

The FIRE movement flaws

The popular but unrealistic, I feel, LeanFIRE or FatFIRE approaches can help tailor your strategy to your retirement goals. LeanFIRE focuses on extreme frugality to retire with a smaller nest egg, while FatFIRE involves saving and investing more aggressively to maintain a higher standard of living (Hester, 2019). By prioritizing smart financial strategies and diversifying my income streams, I'm on the path to achieving FIRE (Financial Independence, Retire Early) and enjoying a fulfilling life on my own terms. Okay, if you're considering living like Charlie from the Chocolate Factory and hoping to find a golden ticket, you might want to reconsider. Living a life of extreme frugality can be like living in a cramped house with all your grandparents, adult kids, and extended family sharing one bed. If you're okay with living like a pauper and giving up life's little luxuries, go ahead. However, such extreme measures might not be necessary or desirable for most people. A balanced approach can provide financial security without sacrificing your quality of life.

"The trouble with retirement is that you never get a day off." —Abe Lemons

In the end, achieving early retirement is possible with careful planning and discipline, such as saving a significant and consistent amount of money while not impacting a comfortable life (Kobliner, 2017; O'Leary, 2018). Investing wisely in diversified index funds, ETFs, and real estate for passive income is crucial (Bogle, 2017; Kiyosaki, 2011). Maximizing tax-advantaged retirement and non-qualified accounts and taking advantage of employer-matching contributions can significantly boost savings (IRS, 2023) as well as the growth of the markets. Embracing multiple income streams through side businesses or freelancing and utilizing tax optimization strategies can accelerate early retirement (Sabin, 2020; Piketty, 2014). Downsizing or moving to a lower-cost-of-living area can reduce expenses while avoiding extreme frugality ensuring a balanced, fulfilling life (Vanderkam, 2015; Hester, 2019). Even though I work in higher education as a Dean of a large School, I prioritize these strategies, disregarding societal expectations, to achieve true financial independence without impacting my enjoyment of life for me or my family.

In conclusion, achieving early retirement is not just a distant dream; it's entirely within reach with the right mix of careful planning, disciplined saving, and strategic investments. By aggressively saving a significant portion of your income, you set the foundation for financial freedom. But remember, it's not just about hoarding money—it's about making smart decisions that align with your goals and values. Whether it's maximizing your savings, investing in diversified assets, or generating multiple income streams, the key is to create a sustainable and enjoyable lifestyle that allows you to retire on your own terms.

"We spend our lives on the run: we get up by the clock, eat and sleep by the clock, get up again, go to work—and then we retire. And what do they give us? A bloody clock!"
—*Dave Allen*

It's also important to debunk the myths around "good debt" and challenge societal norms like the need for a huge house to prove your success. True success is found in financial independence, not in material possessions that drain your resources. Downsizing or moving to a lower-cost area can significantly reduce expenses, making early retirement even more feasible without sacrificing your quality of life.

Healthcare planning is another crucial piece of the puzzle, especially for those retiring before Medicare eligibility. By thoroughly researching your options and regularly reviewing your financial plan, you can ensure that your retirement years are not only financially secure but also free from the stress of unexpected medical costs.

Finally, while the FIRE movement offers some valuable insights, it's important to tailor your retirement strategy to your own needs and desires. Extreme frugality might work for some, but a balanced approach that allows for both financial security and life's little luxuries is often more realistic and fulfilling. By embracing these strategies, you can achieve early retirement and enjoy the freedom to live life on your own terms, long before your peers are even thinking about leaving the workforce.

Chapter 10

Working Towards Retirement Saving

Smart investing is equally crucial. It's not enough to simply save money—you need to make your money work for you. This involves choosing the right mix of investments that match your risk tolerance and time horizon. Diversifying your portfolio across different asset classes, such as stocks, bonds, and real estate, helps manage risk and optimize returns. Understanding how to leverage tax-advantaged accounts, like 401(k)s and IRAs, can also significantly boost your savings by reducing your tax burden and maximizing your investment growth.

My wife and I have always told our kids: start saving early, save consistently, and you'll be able to retire way earlier than most of your friends. But we also remind them that saving every penny to the point of making life hard now isn't the way to go either. Enjoy life, but make sure you're planning for the future too!

"I'm not just retiring from the company; I'm also retiring from my stress, my commute, my alarm clock, and my iron." —Hartman Jule

Together, these elements—strategic planning, disciplined saving, and smart investing—form the foundation of a successful retirement strategy. By carefully balancing these components, you can create a robust financial plan that not only helps you reach your retirement goals but also provides the security and peace of mind to enjoy your golden years to the fullest.

Here are several key strategies to ensure a secure and comfortable retirement:

Start Early and Save Regularly

The sooner you start saving for retirement, the more time your money has to grow. Beginning your savings journey early takes advantage of the power of compound interest, which is essentially earning interest on your interest. This compounding effect accelerates the growth of your savings over time, making even small, regular contributions incredibly impactful.

Regular contributions to retirement accounts, even if they are modest, can accumulate significantly over time. Imagine your retirement savings as a snowball rolling down a hill, gathering more snow and growing larger as it goes. By the time it reaches the bottom, it's a massive snow boulder! This is the magic of compound interest. Starting with a tiny snowflake (or a small contribution), your savings can become an avalanche of wealth by the time you retire.

"I have never liked working. To me a job is an invasion of privacy."
—Danny McGoorty

Setting up automatic transfers to your retirement accounts can help maintain consistency and ensure you are steadily building your nest egg. Automation is like having a financial robot that takes care of your savings while you focus on living your best life. You don't have to remember to transfer money each month, and you reduce the temptation to splurge on that unnecessary gadget or fancy coffee. By automating your savings, you create a disciplined approach to building your retirement fund, ensuring that a portion of your income is always directed toward your future, regardless of other financial demands.

Moreover, automating your savings can provide peace of mind, knowing that you are consistently contributing to your retirement goals. It transforms saving from an optional activity to a guaranteed one, helping to build a robust financial habit. This consistency is key to leveraging the benefits of compound interest fully. As your automated savings grow, you may also find opportunities to increase your contributions over time, further enhancing your retirement fund's growth.

Now, let's sprinkle in the dream of early retirement to this fun financial journey. Imagine clocking out of the office for the last time in your 50s or even your 40s, while your colleagues are still grinding away. By starting early and saving regularly, you're setting yourself up for the ultimate freedom. You could be sipping a margarita on a beach, hiking in the mountains, or finally writing that novel, all while your friends are stuck in yet another never-ending meeting that could've been an email.

The below table shows the retirement savings growth for four individuals, each contributing $250 per month with a 9% annual return, starting at ages 20, 30, 40, and 50 years old. The savings are calculated at 5-year increments up to age 60. This demonstrates the significant impact of starting early on the total accumulated savings due to compound interest. For example, by age 60, the person who started at 20 accumulates approximately $936,264, while the one who started at 50 has about $38,703.

Age	Age savings started			
Age	Age 20	Age 30	Age 40	Age 50
20	-	-	-	-
25	$15,085	-	-	-
30	$38,703	-	-	-
35	$75,681	$15,085	-	-
40	$133,577	$38,703	-	-
45	$224,224	$75,681	$15,085	-
50	$366,149	$133,577	$38,703	-
55	$588,357	$224,224	$75,681	$15,085
60	$936,264	$366,149	$133,577	$38,703

Now, with the same information but, now with the retirement savings contribution of $400 per month with a 9% annual return, starting at ages 20, 30, 40, and 50 years old (table is on next page). The savings are calculated at 5-year increments up to age 60. This demonstrates the significant impact of starting early on the total accumulated savings due to compound interest. For example, by age 60, the person who started at 20 accumulates approximately $1,872,528, while the one who started at 50 has about $77,406.

These tables illustrate the profound effect of starting early when saving for retirement, with a consistent monthly contribution and the magic of compound interest. Picture this: if you start saving $250 per month at age 20, by the time you're 60, you'll be sitting on a mountain of about $936,264. Meanwhile, your friend who started at age 50 will be left holding a measly $38,703, wondering why they ever bought that fancy espresso machine.

But wait, there's more! If you crank up that monthly contribution to $400, the results are even more impressive. Our early bird who started at 20 will have a jaw-dropping $1,872,528 by age 60, while the late bloomer starting at 50 will scrape together about $77,406. It's like comparing a lavish retirement villa in the Caribbean to a tent in your backyard.

	Age savings started			
Age	Age 20	Age 30	Age 40	Age 50
20	-	-	-	-
25	$30,169	-	-	-
30	$77,405	-	-	-
35	$151,362	$30,169	-	-
40	$267,154	$77,405	-	-
45	$448,448	$151,362	$30,169	-
50	$732,297	$267,154	$77,405	-
55	$1,176,713	$448,448	$51,362	$ 30,169
60	$1,872,528	$732,297	$267,154	$ 77,405

These comparisons highlight the critical importance of early and consistent savings to maximize your retirement funds. So start early, save regularly, and let the power of compound interest work its magic. Because nobody wants to be the person at the retirement party who says, "I guess I'll just keep working forever."

Ultimately, the earlier you start saving for retirement, the more you can take advantage of these financial principles. Even small, regular contributions can grow into a significant nest egg, providing financial security and freedom in your retirement years. By automating your savings and committing to consistent contributions, you set the stage for a comfortable and worry-free retirement – and maybe even the chance to retire early and live out your dreams before you turn gray. So, start rolling that snowball today, and let it take you to an early retirement adventure!

Maximize your Retirement Accounts

When thinking about retirement, regardless of your age, preparation is key. It's essential to take full advantage of tax-advantaged retirement accounts such as 401(k)s, IRAs, and Roth IRAs. These accounts are specifically designed to help you save for retirement efficiently, offering various tax benefits that can significantly enhance your savings. By contributing to these accounts, you can reduce your taxable income and benefit from tax-deferred growth, allowing your investments to compound over time without being eroded by taxes. Additionally, Roth IRAs offer the advantage of tax-free withdrawals in retirement, providing a valuable source of income that isn't subject to future tax increases. Ensuring that you maximize your contributions to these accounts each year is a crucial step in building a robust retirement fund that can support you comfortably in your later years. For example, one must look into all possible retirement options, such as:

- **Maximize 401(k) Contributions:** First, if your employer offers a 401(k) plan, contribute enough to receive the full employer match. This match is essentially free money, a benefit that can supercharge your retirement savings. For example, if your employer matches 50% of your contributions up to 6% of your salary, make sure you are contributing at least 6% to capture the full match. This instantly boosts your savings by 50%, a return that's hard to beat in any investment market. Additionally, contributions to a traditional 401(k) are made with pre-tax dollars, reducing your taxable income for the year. This means you can save more aggressively without feeling as much impact on your take-home pay.

62

- **Benefits of Traditional IRAs:** Next, consider contributing to a traditional IRA. Like a 401(k), contributions to a traditional IRA may be tax-deductible, further lowering your taxable income. The money in your IRA grows tax-deferred, meaning you don't pay taxes on the investment gains until you withdraw the money in retirement. This allows your investments to compound more quickly than if they were subject to annual taxes. Traditional IRAs also offer flexibility in investment choices, allowing you to tailor your portfolio to your specific retirement goals and risk tolerance.

- **Roth IRAs for Tax-Free Withdrawals:** Roth IRAs offer a unique advantage: tax-free withdrawals in retirement. Contributions to a Roth IRA are made with after-tax dollars, meaning you don't get a tax break upfront. However, the growth and withdrawals in retirement are completely tax-free, provided certain conditions are met. This can be a significant benefit, especially if you expect to be in a higher tax bracket in retirement. Having a mix of traditional and Roth accounts can provide tax diversification, giving you flexibility to manage your taxable income in retirement.

- **Annuities as a financial tool:** Personally, I do not like annuities and will never own one for a variety of reasons, however, they have their place in the tool kit for retirement. Annuities are financial products designed to provide a steady income stream, typically used as a retirement planning tool. However, the backend costs of annuities can significantly affect their overall value. These costs include various fees such as administrative fees, mortality and expense risk charges, and investment management fees. On average, annuity fees range from 2% to 3% of the account value per year, but they can go higher depending on the specific features and riders selected.

Administrative fees cover the cost of managing the annuity and can range from 0.1% to 0.3% annually. Mortality and expense risk charges, which compensate the insurance company for the risk they take on, generally range from 0.4% to 1.25% annually. Investment management fees, applied to the underlying investments, can add another 0.5% to 2% annually. Additionally, some annuities impose surrender charges if you withdraw funds early, which can be substantial in the initial years of the contract.

Given these significant costs, annuities might not be the best option for the average person. These products are often more beneficial for Certified Financial Planners (CFPs), who gleefully rake in commissions and fees from selling them. Imagine your CFP twirling their mustache as they pocket 2% to 6% on the backend. And if you decide to cancel the annuity, you'll be paying them back for that twirl-worthy commission!

It's crucial to consider whether the high fees and loss of liquidity align with your financial goals. For many individuals, alternative retirement savings vehicles such as IRAs or 401(k)s might be the way to go. These options offer more flexibility and lower costs, ensuring better control over your hard-earned money. So, unless you enjoy watching your CFP do their happy dance while you lose control of your funds, it might be wise to keep those retirement savings where you can see them—and where they aren't funding someone's yacht named "Commission Cruiser."

- **Early Retirement and Tax-Advantaged Accounts:** If early retirement is your goal, these tax-advantaged accounts play a crucial role in your strategy. The earlier you start saving, the more you can leverage the power of compound interest. Even small contributions made consistently over time can grow into a substantial nest egg. For instance, if you start contributing to a 401(k) or IRA in your 20s or 30s, your investments have decades to grow, allowing you to potentially retire in your 50s or even 40s.

- **Strategies for Early Retirement:** To save effectively for early retirement, maximize contributions to your 401(k), taking full advantage of any employer match. Simultaneously, contribute to both traditional and Roth IRAs to balance your tax burden now and in the future. Beyond these accounts, consider other investment vehicles like taxable brokerage accounts, real estate, and Health Savings Accounts (HSAs).

- **My Favorite retirement option, non-qualified mutual funds:** Investing in non-qualified mutual fund accounts offers several benefits for individuals looking to diversify their financial portfolios. These accounts provide greater flexibility compared to qualified accounts, as they are not subject to the same contribution limits and withdrawal restrictions. This means investors can access their funds more easily and can continue to invest significant amounts beyond the caps imposed on retirement accounts. Additionally, non-qualified mutual funds can offer favorable tax treatment on long-term capital gains and dividends, potentially reducing the overall tax burden.

Advantages of Non-Qualified Mutual Fund Accounts

One of the significant advantages of non-qualified mutual fund accounts is the ability to access your money before age 59 1/2 without incurring a penalty, unlike qualified accounts. While you do need to pay taxes on the withdrawals, there are strategies to mitigate this impact. Techniques such as tax-loss harvesting, where you sell losing investments to offset gains, and strategic withdrawals during lower-income years can help manage and minimize tax liabilities. Moreover, by controlling these investments yourself rather than through a firm that takes a cut each quarter, you can avoid management fees that eat into your returns. This self-directed approach allows for a more substantial increase in your growth over time. By incorporating non-qualified mutual fund accounts into their investment strategy, individuals can enjoy increased flexibility, potential tax advantages, and the opportunity to grow their wealth more effectively, providing a robust foundation for financial security and early retirement.

The Resilience of the U.S. Stock Market

The U.S. stock market has demonstrated consistent growth over the past 100 years, despite experiencing fluctuations. Historically, the market has averaged an annual return of around 9-10%, showing resilience and growth over the long term. While there have been periods of significant volatility, including major downturns during events like the Great Depression (1929–1939), the dot-com bubble (2001), and the 2008 financial crisis, these have been balanced by robust periods of recovery and expansion. This long-term upward trend underscores the importance of patience and a steady investment strategy, as even amidst short-term market swings, the overall trajectory has been positive, providing a solid foundation for retirement savings.

Starting Early and Leveraging Tax-Advantaged Accounts

By starting early and making the most of tax-advantaged accounts, you set yourself up for a robust financial future. The combination of employer contributions, tax-deferred growth, and tax-free withdrawals creates a powerful framework for achieving your retirement goals, including the possibility of enjoying an early retirement. With disciplined saving and strategic planning, you can build a substantial nest egg that supports a comfortable and fulfilling retirement lifestyle.

Hilarious Yet Effective Ways to Beef Up Retirement Savings

As you inch closer to retirement, it's time to get serious about making sure your golden years are actually golden, not just a mildly shiny bronze. Here are three hilarious yet effective ways to beef up your retirement savings and lock down that financial future.

1. Catch-Up Contributions: Once you hit the big 5-0, it's time to start throwing extra cash into your retirement accounts like it's

a surprise party and your savings are the guest of honor. Think of it as your financial "second wind," or as I like to call it, "the midlife money crisis."

2. Plan Reviews: Just like you wouldn't let your phone's operating system stay outdated (hello, security breaches and glitches), don't let your retirement plan gather dust. Give it a regular check-up to make sure it's still working as hard as you are. Adjustments might be needed, especially after you've made some impulsive purchases like that hot tub you never use.

3. Diversify Investments: Remember when you thought it was a good idea to put all your Halloween candy in one bag, only to have it confiscated by your dentist? Same principle. Spread your investments around to manage risk and maximize growth. It's like trick-or-treating at the best houses on the block but for your financial portfolio.

Working towards retirement requires a proactive and multifaceted approach—like juggling flaming torches while riding a unicycle. Here's how to master the act without burning your nest egg: Start early. Begin saving as soon as you can. Think of it as planting a money tree. The earlier you plant it, the sooner you can sit in its shade with a fruity drink in hand, laughing at the stock market swings.

Save regularly. Treat your retirement savings like a gym membership—one you actually use. Consistent contributions will bulk up your financial muscles, even if you start with the financial equivalent of lifting soup cans. Maximize retirement accounts. Max out those 401(k)s and IRAs like you're filling up your plate at a buffet. You'll thank yourself later when you're feasting on gains instead of staring at an empty plate.

"Retirement gives you the time literally to recreate yourself through a sport, game or hobby that you always wanted to try or that you haven't done in years." —*Steven Price*

Diversify investments. Don't put all your eggs in one basket. Spread them out, so if one basket gets dropped (thanks, market volatility!), you still have a dozen omelets in the making. Live below your means. Become a coupon-clipping, bargain-hunting ninja. The less you spend now, the more you'll have later to splurge on things like luxury cruises or buying an island—whichever floats your retired boat.

Plan for healthcare costs. Stash away money for those golden years' health expenses. Imagine future you, happily getting those joints replaced or having a top-notch hearing aid, still hearing your grandkids talk about the latest gadget. Pay off debt. Kick debt to the curb like it's that ex who still owes you money. Being debt-free is like hitting the financial jackpot without even buying a ticket.

Regularly review and adjust your plan. Just like you wouldn't let your hairstyle stay stuck in the 80s, don't let your retirement plan gather dust. Of course, as a side note, I loved the ladies' hair back in the 1980s; wish that would come back. Anyway, keep it fresh and up to date to ensure it still fits your fabulous financial goals. By following these strategies, whether you're dreaming of early retirement or sticking to the traditional timeline, you'll be on track to achieve a retirement that's not just secure but downright legendary. Now go forth and conquer those retirement goals like the financial superhero you are!

"Time is more valuable than money. You can get more money, but you cannot get more time." —Jim Rohn

Now, if you and your partner both start saving early and consistently, you can seriously double your retirement numbers, making retirement at 55 not just a possibility, but a breeze. Picture this: each of you saving $250 a month starting at age 20. By the time you're 55, your combined nest egg could buy you not just that swanky beachfront condo, but maybe even the whole beach (~$2,277,340 at 10.7% compounding)! While others are stressing about retirement for the last 10 years, you'll be planning your next adventure. When you both commit to smart saving, you're not just doubling your efforts—you're doubling your freedom and fun in retirement.

Retirement becomes less about pinching pennies and more about living life to the fullest, without a care in the world.

In the grand finale of your retirement planning saga, remember this: saving early and investing smart is like planting a money tree that grows while you sleep, maximizing your 401(k)s and IRAs is akin to loading up at an all-you-can-eat buffet, and regularly reviewing your plan is like updating your wardrobe—nobody wants to be stuck in last decade's financial trends! And don't forget, even when the markets are down and everyone else is running for the hills, you should still be investing. Those downturns are like a clearance sale on stocks and mutual funds, giving you the most potential for gains when the market bounces back. The key to a legendary retirement isn't just about hitting the right numbers; it's about juggling those flaming financial torches with finesse, laughing all the way to the beach where you'll sip margaritas while your money keeps working for you. So, start early, save regularly, invest even in the rough times, and diversify like a pro. By following these hilarious yet effective strategies, you'll be well on your way to a retirement that's not just secure but absolutely epic. Now, go forth and turn those golden years into a full-blown financial fiesta!

Chapter 11

Financial Needs and Costs Before Retirement

A s you inch closer to retirement, it's time to whip out your financial crystal ball and start planning for the costs that will keep you living your best life—because no one wants to spend their golden years pinching pennies and choosing between a cup of coffee or a tank of gas. It's not just about stuffing your mattress with cash; it's about figuring out what you'll actually need and making smart choices to cover those expenses without turning into a financial worrywart.

First up, healthcare—often the sneaky villain of retirement. Those insurance premiums, out-of-pocket costs, and the potential for long-term care can add up faster than you can say "senior discount." Think of it as the ultimate reality check: your body's warranty may expire, but the bills won't. Then there's housing. Whether you're planning to stay in your cozy nest, downsize to something more manageable, or join a retirement community where bingo is a way of life, you'll need to budget carefully.

"If we command our wealth, we shall be rich and free. If our wealth commands us, we are poor indeed."– Edmund Burke

Don't forget about daily living expenses—yes, even in retirement, you still need to eat, keep the lights on, and get from point A to point B. And let's not ignore inflation, the annoying little gremlin that makes everything more expensive as time goes on. Finally, make sure you've got a contingency fund for life's curveballs, like when the roof decides it's had enough or when a surprise medical emergency turns up uninvited.

"I advise you to go on living solely to enrage those who are paying your annuities. It is the only pleasure I have left." — Voltaire

Understanding these costs and preparing for them is your ticket to enjoying retirement without the stress. With a solid plan in place, you can kick back, relax, and focus on more important things—like finally mastering that perfect golf swing or planning your next adventure.

The table below once again shows an income and ductions analysis for the average taxes, retirement, health, and other fees that a typical American pays each month with a gross monthly income of $10,000.

Description	$	Gross Pay %
Federal Tax	1,200	12
State Tax (5%)	500	5
Social Security (6.2%)	620	6.2
Medicare (1.45%)	145	1.45
Health Insurance	800	8
Retirement Contribution	740	7.4
Income before $10,000	$4,005 Total deductions	
	$5,995 Remaining dollars	

The table illustrates that an average American living in a state with a 5% state income tax will only take home approximately 59.9% of their gross pay. This calculation considers various deductions such as federal tax, state tax, Social Security, Medicare, health insurance, and retirement contributions. For instance, from a gross pay of $10,000, significant amounts are deducted for federal tax ($1,200), state tax ($500), Social Security ($620), Medicare ($145), health insurance ($800), and retirement contributions ($740). These deductions total $4,005, leaving a net pay of $5,995, which is about 59.9% of the gross pay. This highlights the substantial impact of mandatory and optional deductions on an individual's take-home pay, underscoring the importance of financial planning and budgeting for everyday living expenses and future retirement savings.

Reevaluating Retirement: You May Need Less

Not to harp of the so-called "Experts" stating that you will need 80% to 90% of your pre-retirement income to maintain your lifestyle in retirement. But hold on a second, does that make sense when most of us are already living on roughly 59% of our gross income after taxes and deductions while working? When you retire, several financial obligations do a disappearing act. Contributions to retirement accounts? Poof, gone. Income taxes? They take a nosedive. Major expenses like mortgage payments? Vanished, especially if you've managed to pay off your home, car, and other obligations (a crucial step for many aiming for a successful retirement). So, unless you plan on picking up a diamond-studded hobby or buying a yacht named "Midlife Crisis," it looks like you might not need to stash away as much as those experts claim. Could it be that they're trying to sell you more so that their commissions go up? Let's be real—peace of mind and a well-planned, sustainable retirement beat a pushy sales pitch any day!

"Retirement is like a long vacation in Las Vegas. The goal is to enjoy it to the fullest, but not so fully that you run out of money."
— Jonathan Clements

Given these reductions, it's feasible to live comfortably on a lower percentage of your pre-retirement income. If you're accustomed to living on 59% of your gross income, aiming to replace 65% to 70% of your pre-retirement income might be sufficient. This adjustment accounts for the essential living expenses you covered while working, with some additional buffer for discretionary spending. So, the whole idea of needing 80% to 90% of your pre-retirement income might be a bit too cautious, especially if you've been a budget wizard and paid off your debts before retiring. Instead of blindly following the expert advice, focus on your actual expenses and how they'll change once you hang up your work boots. If you're used to living on 59% of your income, shooting for 65% to 70% in retirement should let you live well without sacrificing the occasional splurge

72

on grandkid spoiling or those fancy cruises everyone seems to be raving about. Because let's be real, you're already a master at making your paycheck stretch like a yoga instructor, so why not carry that talent into retirement?

"Every time you borrow money, you're robbing your future self."
— *Nathan W. Morris*

If you want to retire at a middle-class level and then start living like a Kardashian, more power to you! But, let's hit pause on that fantasy and return to Earth for a second. Trying to jump from a comfortable, realistic lifestyle to one filled with champagne fountains and designer wardrobes is like trading in your Toyota for a spaceship—totally impractical and destined for a crash landing. Instead of dreaming about luxury cars and private jets, focus on the lifestyle you're used to—one that's grounded in your reality, not in the glitzy unreality of TV shows. Retirement should be about enjoying the freedom you've worked hard for, not stressing over whether you can afford a diamond-encrusted dog collar. So, forget the bling and embrace the joy of a well-planned, sustainable retirement that lets you live comfortably and happily. Remember, peace of mind beats a designer handbag any day—plus, you don't have to worry about it going out of style!

Unmasking Your Annual Retirement Expenses

When planning for retirement, it's crucial to drill down and calculate your true income need, especially if you have no debt. Accurate budgeting becomes essential as your monthly expenses will primarily consist of living costs such as housing, utilities, groceries, transportation, healthcare, and leisure activities. By accurately calculating these expenses, you can develop a realistic retirement budget that reflects your actual needs. Overestimating your income needs can lead to unnecessary stress and excessive saving, potentially reducing your current quality of life, while underestimating can result in financial shortfalls. A precise calculation helps strike the right balance, optimizing your savings strategy to ensure you are neither over-saving nor under-saving for retirement.

"For many people, being asked to solve their own retirement savings problems is like being asked to build their own cars." — Richard Thaler

Knowing your true income needs allows you to determine exactly how much to save and invest, informing your investment strategy. If your needs are lower than expected, you might choose more conservative investments; if higher, you might opt for growth-oriented investments. Additionally, understanding your income needs can help in planning withdrawals from tax-advantaged accounts in a tax-efficient manner, minimizing tax liabilities and maximizing available income. With a clear picture of your income needs, you can plan your retirement lifestyle more effectively, ensuring that you can maintain your desired standard of living without financial worry.

"You can be young without money but you can't be old without it."
— Tennessee Williams

To calculate your true income need, start by identifying essential expenses such as housing, utilities, groceries, transportation, and healthcare, considering inflation for future costs. Include discretionary spending for dining out, entertainment, hobbies, travel, and gifts, which are important for maintaining your quality of life in retirement. Estimate healthcare expenses, including insurance premiums, out-of-pocket costs, and potential long-term care needs, as these often rise with age. Consider the taxes you will owe on different sources of retirement income, including Social Security benefits, pension income, and withdrawals from retirement accounts. Maintain an emergency fund for unexpected expenses, ensuring financial stability even in retirement. Adjust all estimates for inflation to ensure your purchasing power remains stable over time.

"Not having to worry about money is almost like not having to worry about dying."
— Mario Puzo

For example, in the table below, you'll see another proposed monthly budget of $4,900, translating to an annual income after tax of $58,800. That requires a gross income of $73,500 annually ($6,125 per month) before an overall tax rate of 20% is applied. With this precise calculation, you can confidently plan your retirement savings and investments to meet this goal, avoiding financial stress and optimizing your savings while maintaining your desired lifestyle throughout retirement.

Expense	Monthly Amount ($)	Notes
Housing Cost	1200	Taxes and insurance; No mortgage
Utilities	300	Electricity, water, gas, internet, phone
Groceries	600	Food and household supplies
Transportation	400	Fuel, public transport
Healthcare	800	Insurance, out-of-pocket expenses
Insurance	200	Life, health, and other insurance
Entertainment	500	Dining, movies, hobbies
Travel	600	Vacations and trips
Miscellaneous	300	Unexpected expenses
Expenses in Retirement	$4,900	

Sustainable Retirement Income Planning

The table above illustrates that to generate a retirement income of $4,900 monthly ($58,800 annually), you would need a principal investment of $653,333, assuming a 9% growth rate in the market. This calculation is based on the formula for the withdrawal rate, where the annual income needed is divided by the expected rate of return. In this case, dividing $4,900 monthly by 0.09 (9%) gives you the required principal amount of $653,333. This amount ensures that with a consistent 9% return, you can withdraw $4,900 each month without depleting your principal, allowing your investment to sustain your income needs throughout retirement.

"Know what you own, and know why you own it."
— *Peter Lynch*

Finally, as you gear up for retirement, remember this isn't just about cutting out the daily commute and binge-watching Netflix (although that's definitely a perk). It's about making sure your finances are as solid as that chair you'll be sitting in for all those retirement hobbies. Don't be fooled into thinking you'll just coast through retirement on a wave of good vibes and social security checks—planning is key, my friend. You've got to budget for the essentials like healthcare (because those doctor visits don't pay for themselves), housing (whether it's keeping up with the old homestead or downsizing to a swanky senior condo), and daily living expenses (because even in retirement, you still need to eat something other than instant noodles). And let's not forget that emergency fund for when life decides to throw a curveball, like the roof springing a leak or your grandkids convincing you that yes, they really do need that new video game console.

"Cessation of work is not accompanied by cessation of expenses." — Cato

Once you've got it all figured out, you can finally kick back and enjoy the freedom you've worked so hard for. Just remember, planning for retirement is a bit like preparing for a road trip—you can't just pack the snacks and hope for the best. You need a map, a budget for gas, and maybe a spare tire or two. Get your finances in order now, and future you will be high-fiving past you while you're out there living your best retirement life—whether that's traveling the world, perfecting your golf swing, or just finally finishing that stack of books on your nightstand. Retirement might not come with a cape, but with the right plan, it can still be pretty darn super.

Chapter 12

Crafting a Fulfilling Early Retirement

To avoid going stir-crazy with nothing to do in early retirement, it's crucial to plan a smorgasbord of activities that keep you engaged, fulfilled, and socially connected. Think of it as crafting the ultimate bucket list to make every day feel like a weekend!

Start by diving into hobbies you never had time for when work was running your life. Always dreamed of being a rock star? Dust off that old guitar and start strumming—who knows, you might just be the next garage band legend (or at least impress your cat). Feel like channeling your inner Picasso? Grab some paint and a canvas, and don't worry if your first masterpiece looks more like abstract chaos—it's all part of the fun. Or maybe you've always pictured yourself as a master woodworker—now's your chance to create that perfect birdhouse, even if it takes a few wonky tries to get there.

"Something pretty…that's just the surface. People worry so much about aging, but you look younger if you don't worry about it." – Jeanne Moreau

For the outdoor enthusiasts, why not become the neighborhood gardening guru or the next contestant on "The Great Retirement Bake-Off"? Get your hands dirty with some new recipes—who knows, maybe you'll become known for the world's most exotic pancakes (or at least the most interesting attempts). Keep your body in motion by joining a gym or taking yoga classes. If the thought of lifting weights makes you yawn, hop on a bike and cycle around town like a kid with no curfew. Or, join a recreational sports league and discover the joy of pickleball—yes, it's a real thing, and yes, it's surprisingly addictive!

Volunteering is another great way to keep busy and feel good about yourself. Offer your time at local charities, food banks, or animal shelters. Unleash your inner wise owl by mentoring the youth or dive into community clean-up events like the superhero you always knew you were. If travel is your thing, start exploring nearby attractions and take road trips that make you feel like you're on an endless vacation. Don't just stick to the familiar—venture out and get lost (in a good way) in new cities, states, or even countries. You might just come back with a collection of quirky souvenirs and stories that will make your friends green with envy.

Staying socially engaged is key to avoiding that dreaded retirement boredom. Join clubs that match your interests, attend local meetups, or host epic family gatherings that become the stuff of legends. Keep your brain buzzing with classes, online courses, or workshops. Set ambitious reading goals, learn a new language (and casually show off at the local café), or become the crossword puzzle master you always wanted to be.

If you're feeling entrepreneurial, consider dabbling in part-time work or starting a small business based on your passions. Offer your skills on a freelance basis, or try gig work like driving for a rideshare service—after all, your car, your rules! And finally, focus on personal growth. Meditate, practice mindfulness, and stay zen. Eat well, stay healthy, and maybe even join a spiritual community. By planning a buffet of activities that resonate with you, you'll ensure your early retirement is packed with excitement, meaning, and a whole lot of fun, keeping boredom at bay and your spirits high.

Now, let's get real for a second. The reality of achieving a successful retirement at any age is entirely within reach—with the right planning and a pinch of common sense. Steer clear of burdensome debts like mortgages, car loans, and student loans (because, let's face it, no one wants to be paying off a car when they're 80). Keep a realistic perspective on your retirement expenses and plan accordingly. The secret to a thriving retirement isn't hoping to spend less, but ensuring your financial strategy accommodates a lifestyle that's both fulfilling and sustainable. With careful preparation and disciplined financial management, you can retire confidently, comfortably, and maybe even a little bit earlier than you thought. So go ahead, embrace your inner planner, and get ready to live your best life—because retirement is just the beginning of the fun!

Retirement doesn't have to be expensive to be fulfilling and fun. Here are five affordable activities that will help you stay active, engaged, and enjoying life without straining your budget. Here are some fun things to do when retired:

- **Pick Up a New Hobby** – Dive into something you've always wanted to try but never had the time for, like painting, photography, woodworking, or even learning a musical instrument.

- **Volunteer for a Cause You Love** – Retirement is a great time to give back. Whether it's working with animals, mentoring youth, or helping out at a community garden, volunteering offers both fulfillment and the opportunity to meet new people.

- **Start a Side Hustle or Passion Project** – Have a knack for something? Turn your hobbies or interests into a fun side business, like selling handmade crafts online or becoming a local tour guide in your town.

- **Get Active and Stay Fit** – Join a hiking group, take up golf, or sign up for yoga and tai chi classes. Staying physically active keeps you healthy, energized, and offers a social outlet with others who share the same goals.

- **Explore Local Parks and Hiking Trails** – You don't need to spend a fortune to enjoy the outdoors. Take advantage of local parks, hiking trails, and nature reserves. Many communities have beautiful spots to explore, perfect for picnics, walking, or birdwatching.

Chapter 13

The Viability of Early Retirement

In this chapter, I will dive into how early retirement is not just a pipe dream but totally doable with the right habits and strategies. Early retirement is a viable option for those who plan and prepare carefully. It involves strategic financial planning, disciplined saving, and smart investing to ensure that one's nest egg is sufficient to support a long, fulfilling retirement. Those who retire early often enjoy numerous benefits, such as increased freedom to pursue passions, improved health due to reduced stress, and more time for personal growth, hobbies, and family connections. By addressing and dispelling common myths and fears surrounding early retirement, such as the misconception that it is only for the ultra-wealthy or that it leads to boredom, more people can see that early retirement is not just a dream but an achievable goal. With the right approach, individuals can craft a retirement plan that allows them to live comfortably and pursue their interests without the constraints of traditional employment. Whether through living frugally, maximizing retirement accounts, or generating passive income, a fulfilling and financially secure retirement is within reach for those who are diligent and proactive in their planning.

Saving for early retirement

Starting to save early and harnessing the magic of compound interest is like planting a money tree that keeps growing while you sleep. The real beauty of compound interest? It's like getting paid to do nothing—because once your interest starts earning interest, your money practically does cartwheels, doubling and tripling itself over time. It's the financial equivalent of a snowball rolling downhill, except instead of getting buried, you end up buried in cash. So, start early, sit back, and let compound interest do the heavy lifting while you kick back and enjoy the show! By consistently setting aside even a modest amount each month—say $200— you can significantly enhance your financial future. For example, if you invest $200 monthly at a projected annual return of 9%, your contributions will grow substantially over time, far beyond the simple sum of your deposits (see table).

Age	Additions per year	Savings age 22	Savings age 42
22	$2,400	$2,400	-
27	$2,400	$15,085	-
32	$2,400	$38,703	-
37	$2,400	$75,681	-
42	$2,400	$133,577	$2,400
47	$2,400	$224,224	$15,085
52	$2,400	$366,149	$38,703
57	$2,400	$588,357	$75,681

The above information is something I've hammered into my kids from day one: saving as early as possible is the golden ticket to a comfortable and significant retirement by the age of 55. I've made it clear that if they start young, they'll be in a prime position to enjoy life and retire without a worry in the world. And even if they wait until 65 to really ramp up their savings, they'll still be in a solid spot to enjoy their golden years without financial stress.

"Men do not quit playing because they grow old; they grow old because they quit playing." —Oliver Wendell Holmes

But here's the kicker—I've always told them that retirement planning isn't like studying for a school test where you can just cram the night before and hope for a miracle. You can't pull an all-nighter, chugging coffee and crunching numbers, and expect to magically ace retirement. Treating it like a last-minute rush job is a one-way ticket to Flop City. The secret sauce is all about starting early and being consistent, so they're not stuck trying to frantically catch up when they should be out there living their best lives. It's like planting a money tree—you've got to water it now, so it's giving you shade and fruit later, not leaving you sweating bullets under the hot sun of financial stress.

The earlier you begin saving, the longer your money has to grow, and the more powerful the effect of compound interest becomes. Each dollar saved today is worth significantly more in the future because it has more time to benefit from compounding. This strategy allows small, regular contributions to accumulate into a substantial financial cushion, providing security and flexibility in the future. Over decades, this disciplined approach to saving can turn what seems like modest contributions into a robust nest egg, giving you the financial freedom to retire early, pursue passions, or simply enjoy peace of mind knowing you have a solid financial foundation. This approach doesn't require a high income or extraordinary investment acumen—just consistency, patience, and time working in your favor.

"It's time to say goodbye, but I think goodbyes are sad, and I'd much rather say hello. Hello to a new adventure." —Ernie Harwell

By adopting disciplined saving practices, making wise investment choices, and living below your means, you can build a substantial financial cushion that lets you wave goodbye to the rat race well before the traditional timeline. I'll dish out practical advice, real-life examples, and step-by-step plans to guide you on your journey to sipping margaritas while your friends are still stuck in meetings. With determination and a clear strategy, you can turn the dream of early retirement into your fabulous reality.

Ultimately, financial advisors, including many big-name financial gurus, may not have your best interest at heart when dispensing retirement advice. Often, their primary goal is to fund their retirements by selling you their books, courses, commissions, and advisory services. These "experts" can sometimes prioritize their profits over providing unbiased, personalized financial guidance. While their advice may contain general truths, it's important to remember that their ultimate success hinges on convincing you to buy their products. This can lead to a one-size-fits-all approach that doesn't necessarily align with your unique financial situation and retirement goals.

In the end, when you sit down with a financial advisor, don't walk in like a deer in headlights, they will see that and do what they can for their own personal commissions. Arm yourself with some knowledge first—know what your goals are and have a basic understanding of investment vehicles like mutual funds, stocks, and annuities. This way, you won't get caught up in a sales pitch designed to pad their commission. Remember, your financial future is the main event, and you're the one in the driver's seat—don't let anyone steer you off course!

Chapter 14

Pathways to Early Retirement: Beyond FIRE

A realistic early retirement strategy, distinct from the FIRE method, emphasizes traditional financial planning with strategic enhancements. Start by establishing a solid financial foundation: build a robust emergency fund covering 6-12 months of expenses and manage debt, particularly high-interest debt, to reduce financial strain and free up resources for saving and investing. Consistently save by maximizing contributions to employer-sponsored retirement plans, such as 401(k)s, and IRAs, taking full advantage of employer matching. Set up automatic transfers to ensure regular contributions to retirement and investment accounts.

"Don't act your age in retirement. Act like the inner young person you have always been." – J. A. West

Invest in a diversified portfolio tailored to your risk tolerance and time horizon, including stocks, bonds, and real estate for rental income and appreciation. Utilize tax-efficient strategies and accounts to minimize tax liabilities. Define clear retirement goals, encompassing your desired lifestyle, location, and activities, and use financial planning tools or consult a financial advisor to create projections and adjust plans as needed. Develop multiple income streams, such as part-time work, freelance opportunities, or side businesses, and invest in assets that generate passive income, like dividends, interest, and rental properties.

Healthcare planning is crucial; if eligible, contribute to a Health Savings Account (HSA) to save for medical expenses with tax advantages, and plan for healthcare costs in retirement, including Medicare and supplemental insurance. Maintain a disciplined budget and live within your means, considering downsizing your home or relocating to a more affordable area to reduce living expenses. Stay informed about financial markets, retirement planning strategies, and tax laws to make informed decisions, and periodically consult with a financial advisor to review and adjust your retirement plan. By combining these strategies, you can create a realistic and sustainable early retirement plan without strictly adhering to the FIRE method, maintaining flexibility to adapt as your circumstances and goals evolve.

Solid Financial Foundation

A realistic early retirement strategy, distinct from the FIRE method, emphasizes traditional financial planning with strategic enhancements. Start by establishing a solid financial foundation. For instance, John and Sarah, a couple in their 30s, built an emergency fund covering 12 months of living expenses by automating their savings to set aside $500 each month until they reached their goal of $30,000. Similarly, Maria, a software engineer, prioritized paying off her high-interest credit card debt. She used the snowball method, focusing on her smallest debt first while making minimum payments on others, eventually becoming debt-free within three years.

"I can't change the direction of the wind, but I can adjust my sails to always reach my destination." – Jimmy Dean

Consistent saving is crucial. Kevin, a marketing manager, contributes the maximum allowed to his 401(k) plan and takes full advantage of his employer's 5% matching program. Additionally, he contributes to a Roth IRA annually. Jane, a graphic designer, set up automatic transfers to her retirement and investment accounts, ensuring she saves 20% of her income each month without fail. Here are some basic strategies that you can use to save for your future:

- **Debt Management:** Prioritized paying off high-interest credit card debt. Use the snowball method, focusing on the smallest debt first while making minimum payments on others, eventually becoming debt-free within three years.
- **Maximize Retirement Accounts:** Contributes the maximum allowed to his 401(k) plan and takes full advantage of the employer's 5% matching program. Additionally, contribute to a Roth IRA annually.
- **Regular Contributions:** Set up automatic transfers to retirement and investment accounts and try to save 20% of income each month without fail.

Diversified Investments

Investing in a diversified portfolio tailored to your risk tolerance and time horizon is another key step. One should maintain a diversified investment portfolio with a mix of 60% stocks and 40% bonds, regularly rebalancing to maintain desired allocation as one nears retirement. One of my not so favorites is, investing in a rental property in a growing neighborhood, generating consistent rental income and seeing significant appreciation over the past five years. If possible, use tax-efficient strategies like investing in municipal bonds for tax-free income and contributing to a Health Savings Account (HSA) for tax-advantaged medical savings. Here are some other ideas for diversification:

- **Real Estate:** Emily, a nurse, invested in a rental property in a growing neighborhood. The property generates consistent rental income and has appreciated significantly over the past five years.
- **Tax-Efficient Investments:** David, a financial analyst, uses tax-efficient strategies like investing in municipal bonds for tax-

free income and contributing to a Health Savings Account (HSA) for tax-advantaged medical savings.

Long-Term Planning

This involves defining clear retirement goals, which encompass various aspects such as desired lifestyle, location, and activities. For example, you might envision a retirement where you travel extensively, engage in volunteer work, or pursue hobbies and interests that you didn't have time for during your working years. It's important to detail what your ideal retirement looks like so you can create a financial plan tailored to achieving these specific goals.

"For many, retirement is a time for personal growth, which becomes the path to greater freedom." —*Robert Delamontague*

Consider the location where you want to retire. Some may choose to stay in their current home, while others might prefer moving to a different city or country that offers a lower cost of living, better climate, or proximity to family and friends. The choice of location can significantly impact your cost of living and, consequently, your savings and investment strategy.

In addition to lifestyle and location, consider the activities you plan to engage in during retirement. Whether it's traveling, taking up new hobbies, or continuing education, these activities will require funding. Planning for these costs ahead of time helps ensure you can enjoy your retirement without financial stress.

Using financial planning software is an effective way to project your retirement needs. These tools allow you to input various factors, such as your current savings, expected retirement age, projected expenses, and anticipated income sources. The software can then provide estimates of how much you need to save and invest to reach your retirement goals. It can also help identify any shortfalls and suggest adjustments to your savings rate or investment strategy.

Regularly consulting with a financial advisor is crucial in long-term planning. An advisor can provide personalized advice based on your unique financial situation and goals. They can help you navigate complex issues such as tax planning, investment choices, and withdrawal strategies. Moreover, they can assist in making necessary adjustments to your plan as your circumstances change, whether due to market fluctuations, changes in income, or shifts in your retirement goals.

By defining clear retirement goals, utilizing financial planning tools, and seeking professional advice, you can create a robust long-term plan. This approach ensures you stay on track and make informed adjustments, ultimately achieving a fulfilling and financially secure retirement

Income Streams

Developing multiple income streams is a realistic and beneficial strategy for early retirement, as it reduces reliance on a single source of income and provides financial stability. Diversification can be achieved through a variety of approaches tailored to individual skills and interests.

One practical approach is taking on part-time consulting work. For instance, if you have expertise in a specific field, you can offer your services to companies on a project basis. This not only provides additional income but also allows for flexible working hours that can accommodate a semi-retired lifestyle. Teaching online courses is another viable option. Many professionals with specialized knowledge create and sell courses on platforms like Udemy, Coursera, or Teachable, generating income from course sales while helping others learn valuable skills.

"And in the end it's not the years in your life that count. It's the life in your years."
—Abraham Lincoln

Freelance projects are another excellent way to diversify income. Platforms such as Upwork, Fiverr, and Freelancer enable you to offer a wide range of services, from writing and graphic design to programming and virtual assistance. This flexibility allows you to take on projects that fit your schedule and interests, providing a steady flow of income.

Investing in dividend-paying stocks and bonds is a proven method to generate passive income. Dividends from stocks can provide regular income without the need to sell investments, while interest from bonds offers a reliable income stream with lower risk compared to stocks. It's important to build a diversified portfolio that balances growth and income, aligning with your risk tolerance and retirement timeline.

Additionally, real estate can be a significant source of income. Owning rental properties can provide consistent monthly rental income and potential property appreciation over time. For those who prefer less hands-on involvement, investing in Real Estate Investment Trusts (REITs) offers exposure to real estate markets without the need to manage physical properties.

Another income stream to consider is creating a small business or side hustle based on a personal passion or hobby. This could range from selling handmade crafts online to starting a blog or YouTube channel that generates ad revenue and sponsorships. These ventures can start small and grow over time, providing both financial rewards and personal fulfillment.

Lastly, consider generating income through intellectual property, such as writing a book, composing music, or creating software. Royalties and licensing fees from these creative endeavors can provide long-term income with minimal ongoing effort once the initial work is completed.

> *"You are never too old to set a new goal or dream a new dream."*
> —C.S. Lewis

By diversifying income streams through consulting work, online teaching, freelancing, dividend-paying investments, real estate, small businesses, and intellectual property, you can create a robust financial foundation. This approach not only supplements retirement savings but also offers flexibility and resilience against economic fluctuations, ensuring a more secure and enjoyable early retirement.

Healthcare Planning

Healthcare planning is crucial for ensuring financial security during retirement, given the rising costs of medical care and the potential for unexpected health issues. One effective strategy is contributing to a Health Savings Account (HSA). HSAs offer a triple tax advantage: contributions are made with pre-tax dollars, the money grows tax-free, and withdrawals for qualified medical expenses are also tax-free. By regularly contributing to an HSA, you can build a substantial nest egg specifically earmarked for healthcare expenses. Additionally, many HSAs offer investment options that allow your contributions to grow over time, further increasing your savings.

When planning for healthcare costs in retirement, it's important to understand and enroll in Medicare, the federal health insurance program for people aged 65 and older. Medicare has several parts: Part A (hospital insurance), Part B (medical insurance), Part C (Medicare Advantage plans), and Part D (prescription drug coverage). While Part A is usually premium-free, Parts B, C, and D may require premiums. It's crucial to budget for these costs and select the coverage that best fits your healthcare needs.

Supplemental insurance policies, such as Medigap, can cover expenses that Medicare does not, including copayments, coinsurance, and deductibles. Medigap plans are standardized and sold by private insurance companies, providing additional financial protection and peace of mind. By purchasing a Medigap policy, you can reduce out-of-pocket expenses and avoid unexpected medical bills.

Long-term care insurance is another consideration for comprehensive healthcare planning. This type of insurance covers services that Medicare typically does not, such as assistance with daily living activities (bathing, dressing, eating) either at home or in a long-term care facility. Given the high cost of long-term care, having insurance can prevent significant financial strain and protect your retirement savings.

> *"Don't simply retire from something; have something to retire to."*
> —*Harry Emerson Fosdick*

It's also wise to explore the options and benefits of employer-sponsored retiree health benefits if available. Some employers offer health insurance coverage for retirees, which can be a valuable supplement to Medicare and reduce overall healthcare costs.

Regularly reviewing and updating your healthcare plan is essential, as health needs and financial situations can change over time. Staying informed about changes in Medicare, insurance policies, and healthcare costs will enable you to make adjustments as necessary. Consulting with a financial advisor who specializes in retirement and healthcare planning can provide personalized guidance and help you navigate complex decisions.

By contributing to an HSA, enrolling in Medicare, purchasing supplemental insurance policies, considering long-term care insurance, and exploring employer-sponsored benefits, you can create a comprehensive healthcare plan. This approach ensures that you are financially prepared for medical expenses, allowing you to enjoy a more secure and stress-free retirement.

Lifestyle Adjustments

Lifestyle adjustments are vital for a successful early retirement strategy, helping ensure that your financial resources are aligned with your retirement goals. Maintaining a disciplined budget and living within your means are foundational elements of this process. One effective budgeting method is the 50/30/20 rule. While I get that the 50/30/20 rule is like trying to fit a square peg into a round hole—overly simplistic and ignoring individual financial situations and personal and family life circumstances—making it an ineffective strategy for many seeking early retirement, we'll discuss it now, so the enthusiasts don't flood my inbox with complaints. Therefore, this guideline suggests allocating 50% of your income to necessities such as housing, utilities, groceries, and transportation. Another 30% should go towards discretionary spending, which includes dining out, entertainment, vacations, and other non-essential purchases. The remaining 20% should be dedicated to savings and debt repayment, ensuring that you are consistently building your financial reserves and reducing liabilities.

"I see retirement as just another of these reinventions, another chance to do new things and be a new version of myself." —Walt Mossberg

Implementing the 50/30/20 rule requires tracking your income and expenses like a hawk. Use budgeting tools and apps to monitor your spending habits—think of them as your financial surveillance squad. Regularly review your budget to make sure it aligns with your current financial situation and goals, because, let's face it, life happens. By sticking to this rule, you'll avoid overspending and ensure a chunk of your income goes toward savings and debt reduction, both of which are critical for your early retirement dreams—assuming your avocado toast addiction doesn't derail everything.

Another significant lifestyle adjustment is considering downsizing from a large family home to a smaller, more affordable property. As children move out and your need for space decreases, selling your larger home and purchasing a smaller one can significantly reduce your living expenses. This move can lower costs associated with mortgage payments, property taxes, utilities, and maintenance. The equity released from selling a larger home can be invested to boost your retirement savings or pay off any remaining debt.

In addition to downsizing your home, explore other ways to reduce expenses. This might include cutting back on non-essential services like premium cable packages, gym memberships, or frequent dining out. Consider adopting a more minimalist lifestyle, focusing on experiences and activities that bring joy and fulfillment without substantial costs. For example, instead of expensive vacations, you might opt for local trips, hiking, or other low-cost recreational activities.

Transportation is another area where adjustments can yield significant savings. Evaluate whether you need multiple vehicles or if you can downsize to one car. Opting for a fuel-efficient or used vehicle instead of a new, high-end model can also save money. Additionally, exploring public transportation options, biking, or walking can further reduce transportation costs and contribute to a healthier lifestyle.

"Living each day as if it were your last doesn't mean your last day of retirement on a remote island. It means to live fully, authentically and spontaneously with nothing being held back." —Jack Canfield

Healthcare and insurance expenses are crucial components of your budget. Research and choose cost-effective healthcare plans that provide adequate coverage without excessive premiums. Utilize preventive care services to maintain your health and avoid costly medical treatments. Additionally, regularly review your insurance policies, including auto, home, and life insurance, to ensure you are not overpaying and have the appropriate coverage for your needs.

Moreover, consider supplementing your income with part-time work or side gigs that align with your interests and skills. This not only provides additional funds but also keeps you engaged and active. Freelancing, consulting, tutoring, or even turning a hobby into a small business can be fulfilling ways to generate extra income without committing to full-time employment.

Maintaining a disciplined budget, downsizing your home, cutting non-essential expenses, and exploring additional income opportunities are key lifestyle adjustments that support a realistic early retirement strategy. By making these changes, you can reduce financial stress, allocate more funds to retirement savings, and enjoy a more secure and fulfilling retirement.

Continual Education

Continual education and staying informed about financial markets, retirement planning strategies, and tax laws are vital components of a successful early retirement plan. The financial landscape is constantly evolving, with new investment opportunities, changing regulations, and emerging economic trends that can significantly impact your retirement strategy. To stay ahead, regularly read financial news and blogs from reputable sources. This helps you understand the latest market movements, investment strategies, and economic forecasts. Subscribing to newsletters from financial experts can provide valuable insights and tips.

"A retired husband is often a wife's full-time job." —Ella Harris

Attending webinars and online courses is another excellent way to deepen your financial knowledge. Many financial institutions, investment firms, and educational platforms offer free or low-cost webinars on various topics, such as retirement planning, tax optimization, and portfolio management. Online courses can provide a more comprehensive understanding of complex subjects, allowing you to make more informed decisions about your financial future. Websites like Coursera, Udemy, and

Khan Academy offer a wide range of finance-related courses that you can complete at your own pace.

Periodically consulting with a financial advisor is essential to ensure your retirement plan remains aligned with your goals. A professional advisor can provide personalized advice based on your unique financial situation, helping you navigate changes in the market and adjust your strategy as needed. They can assist with tax planning, investment choices, and withdrawal strategies, ensuring you make the most of your retirement savings. Regular check-ins with your advisor can help you stay on track and make necessary adjustments, whether it's reallocating assets, updating your budget, or modifying your savings goals.

Additionally, joining financial communities or forums can be beneficial. Engaging with others who share similar retirement goals can provide support, encouragement, and valuable insights. These communities often share real-life experiences, tips, and strategies that you might not find in traditional financial news sources.

"When a [person] retires and time is no longer a matter of urgent importance, [their] colleagues generally present [them] with a watch." —R.C. Sheriff

By combining these strategies—regularly reading financial news, attending webinars and courses, consulting with a financial advisor, and participating in financial communities—you can create a realistic and sustainable early retirement plan. This approach allows you to stay informed and adapt your plan as circumstances and goals evolve, ensuring that you are prepared for any financial challenges that may arise. Ultimately, maintaining flexibility and staying proactive in your financial education will help you achieve a secure and fulfilling early retirement without relying solely on the FIRE method.

Chapter 15

Planning for Early Retirement

Retirement is often that elusive mirage on the horizon, a distant dream where you finally get to trade in your alarm clock for a life of leisure—assuming you can figure out how to survive without a paycheck. But for those brave souls who've decided they want to hit the retirement button by age 55 (because who wants to wait until their hair turns fully gray?), the stakes are even higher. You've got to channel your inner financial wizard, meticulously planning and strategizing like you're plotting a heist in a blockbuster movie.

"The trouble with retirement is that you never get a day off."
– Abe Lemons

The big question is: how much cash do you need to stash away to make sure you're not living off ramen noodles and tap water? This is where things get serious—well, as serious as calculating future expenses can be when you're still trying to figure out what you're having for dinner tonight. This section will walk you through the nuts and bolts of figuring out your retirement magic number, so you can retire early and still afford to spoil your grandkids rotten.

We'll dive into different retirement age scenarios and even throw in a little inflation adjustment because, let's face it, prices rise faster than your nephew's excitement over a new video game. With this guide, you'll be equipped to map out your early retirement with the confidence of someone who knows exactly how much sunscreen to pack for their permanent vacation. While I do not prescribe to the arbitrary formula, I will show you how to use it if you are a true believer. Therefore, here is a method to use calculate your retirement figure starting at age 55:

1. Estimate Your Annual Retirement Expenses
- List Current Expenses: List all your current monthly and annual expenses.
- Adjust for Retirement: Estimate how these expenses might change in retirement.
- Include Lifestyle Choices: Account for any new hobbies, travel, or lifestyle changes.

2. Calculate the Desired Annual Retirement Income
Determine how much income you'll need each year in retirement based on your estimated annual expenses. Aim for 70-80% of your pre-retirement income as a general rule, but adjust according to your personal circumstances.

3. Determine Your Withdrawal Rate
A common safe withdrawal rate is 4%, which helps ensure you don't outlive your savings over a 30-year period, however, I personally do not prescribe to this method.

4. Calculate the Total Retirement Savings Needed
Use the following formula to calculate the total retirement savings required:

$$\text{Required Savings} = \frac{\text{Desired Annual Income}}{\text{Safe Withdrawal Rate}}$$

5. Adjust for Inflation
Consider the impact of inflation on your retirement expenses:

$$\text{Future Value} = \text{Present Value} \times (1 + \text{Inflation Rate})^{\text{Number of Years}}$$

Example Calculation Starting at Age 55

- **Estimate Annual Expenses**: Suppose your estimated annual retirement expenses are $60,000.
- **Desired Annual Income**: Based on your expenses, your desired annual income is $60,000.
- **Withdrawal Rate**: Using the 4% rule.
- **Calculate Required Savings**:

$$\text{Required Savings} = \frac{60,000}{0.04} = 1,500,000$$

This means you need $1.5 million in savings to generate $60,000 annually.

6. **Adjust for Inflation**: If you plan to retire at age 55 and you are currently 35 years old (20 years until retirement) with an expected 2% annual inflation rate:

$$\text{Future Annual Expenses} = 60,000 \times (1 + 0.02)^{20} \approx 89,852$$

$$\text{Future Required Savings} = \frac{89,852}{0.04} \approx 2,246,300$$

So, you would need approximately $2.25 million to retire at age 55 with the equivalent purchasing power of $60,000 today.

7. Plan for Different Scenarios

It's beneficial to plan for various scenarios by adjusting:

- **Retirement Age**: Calculate how retiring earlier or later affects your required savings.
- **Investment Returns**: Consider both conservative and optimistic return scenarios.
- **Life Expectancy**: Plan for a longer retirement to ensure you don't outlive your savings.

Calculating your retirement doesn't need to feel like solving a complex math problem (fuzzy math) from outer space—it's really just basic math with a side of common sense. If you can figure out how many pizzas you need for a party, you can handle this! Forget the fuzzy math meant to freak you out; saving for retirement is as simple as adding, subtracting, and making sure your future self can afford all the snacks.

Explanation of the Retirement Planning Table

The table provides a detailed calculation of the savings required to retire at various ages, starting at age 55, with a desired annual retirement income of $80,000. The table factors in an annual inflation rate of 2% and uses a 4% safe withdrawal rate, which is a common guideline for sustainable withdrawals from retirement savings. Within this example (Table) the key columns are:

1. **Retirement Age**: The age at which you plan to retire.

2. **Years in Retirement**: The number of years you expect to be in retirement, calculated based on a life expectancy of 90 years.

3. **Required Annual Income**: The desired annual income during retirement, set at $80,000 for this example.

4. **Future Value of Annual Income** (Adjusted for Inflation): The future value of the desired annual income, adjusted for inflation. This shows how much $80,000 today will be worth at the time of retirement, considering the 2% annual inflation rate.

5. **Required Savings**: The total amount of savings required at the time of retirement to provide the future value of the desired annual income using a 4% withdrawal rate.

Savings Starting at 55

Retirement Age	Years in Retirement	Adjusted for Inflation	Required Savings
55	35	$118,875	$2,971,895
60	30	$131,248	$3,281212
65	25	$144,908	$3,622,723
70	20	$159,991	$3,999,779
75	15	$176,643	$4,416,079

Detailed Explanation for Information in the Table

The table offers a detailed analysis of the required savings at various ages, from 55 to 75, to ensure a secure retirement. It highlights how the amount you need to retire comfortably increases as you delay retirement, emphasizing the importance of early and consistent saving.

- **Retirement Age 55**:
  - Years in Retirement: 35 (90 - 55)
  - Future Value of Annual Income: $118,875.79
    - Calculated as $80,000 * $(1+0.02)^{20}$ to account for 20 years of inflation.
  - Required Savings: $2,971,895
    - Calculated as $118,875.79 / 0.04.
- **Retirement Age 60**:
  - Years in Retirement: 30 (90 - 60)
  - Future Value of Annual Income: $131,248.48
    - Calculated as $80,000 * $(1+0.02)$ x 25 to account for 25 years of inflation.
  - Required Savings: $3,281,212
    - Calculated as $131,248.48 / 0.04.
- **Retirement Age 65**:
  - Years in Retirement: 25 (90 - 65)
  - Future Value of Annual Income: $144,908.93
    - Calculated as $80,000 * $(1 | 0.02)^{30}$ to account for 30 years of inflation.
  - Required Savings: $3,622,723
    - Calculated as $144,908.93 / 0.04.

- **Retirement Age 70**:
    - Years in Retirement: 20 (90 - 70)
    - Future Value of Annual Income: $159,991.16
        - Calculated as $80,000 * $(1+0.02)^{35}$ to account for 35 years of inflation.
    - Required Savings: $3,999,779
        - Calculated as $159,991.16 / 0.04.
- **Retirement Age 75**:
    - Years in Retirement: 15 (90 - 75)
    - Future Value of Annual Income: $176,643.17
        - Calculated as $80,000 * $(1+0.02)^{40}$ to account for 40 years of inflation.
    - Required Savings: $4,416,079
        - Calculated as $176,643.17 / 0.04.

The above table and data illustrates how inflation impacts the future value of your desired annual income and how much you need to save to retire comfortably at different ages. It highlights the importance of accounting for inflation and demonstrates the impact of different retirement ages on the total savings required. By understanding these figures, you can better plan and strategize your savings to ensure a secure and financially stable retirement.

> *"There's never enough time to do all the nothing you want."*
> *— Bill Waterson, Calvin & Hobbes*

The 4% retirement withdrawal rule is often touted as a reliable guideline, but it's essentially a blanket approach that doesn't fully account for the complexities of the real world. It assumes a steady, predictable market and a one-size-fits-all lifestyle, which is rarely the case. In reality, market conditions fluctuate, sometimes drastically, and people's life expectations vary widely—from healthcare costs to personal goals and unforeseen expenses. Relying solely on the 4% rule can lead to either an overly conservative approach, potentially leaving money on the table, or an overly optimistic one, risking running out of funds too soon. A more personalized, flexible strategy is essential to truly meet individual needs and adapt to the unpredictable nature of both the market and life itself.

Understanding Your Retirement Needs: Balancing Annual Income with Investment Returns

The table below provides a clear representation of the funds required to retire comfortably, assuming an annual need of $80,000, adjusted for a 2% average inflation rate over a 30-year retirement. By considering an average market growth rate of 9%, the table illustrates the relationship between the desired yearly income during retirement and the total savings needed to generate that income. Unlike the traditional 4% rule, which is over 30 years old and may not fully account for modern economic conditions, this example offers a more tailored approach.

Just to let you know over the past 50 years, the U.S. stock market has delivered impressive average annual returns. The Dow Jones Industrial Average (DJIA) has grown by approximately 8-9% per year, while the S&P 500 has averaged around 10-11% annually. The NASDAQ Composite, known for its tech-heavy focus, has led the way with an average return of about 10-12% per year. These historical averages underscore the potential for long-term growth in the stock market, though it's important to remember that individual year-to-year returns can vary significantly. Firstly, let's be real—markets are like a rollercoaster with periods of wild highs and stomach-churning lows. So, when we talk about averages, like the ones above and below, we're smoothing out the crazy ride. You can't just live for the lows, clutching your pearls every time the market dips. You've got to embrace the highs too—because it's the overall journey that counts, not just the bumps along the way!

Alright, let's focus on the specific needs and potential returns relevant to today's retirement planning. This ensures that your retirement plan is both realistic and aligned with potential investment returns, allowing you to maintain your desired lifestyle throughout your retirement years.

Douglas B Sims

Retirement Age	Retirement Years	Adjusted for Inflation	Required Savings at Retirement
55	35	$118,875	$1,320,833
60	30	$131,248	$1,458,311
65	25	$144,908	$1,610,089
70	20	$159,991	$1,77,678
75	15	$176,643	$1,962,700

This table simplifies the often-daunting process of retirement planning by breaking down the essential calculations into easy-to-understand figures. By focusing on the relationship between your desired annual retirement income and the total savings required, the table provides a clear roadmap for how much you need to save to maintain your lifestyle throughout your retirement.

"Retirement is like a long vacation in Las Vegas. The goal is to enjoy it the fullest, but not so fully that you run out of money." – Jonathan Clements

For example, if your goal is to have an annual income of $118,875 during retirement, this table shows that you'll need to achieve a 9% return on your investments, factoring in an average 2% inflation rate over 30 years. It's important to note that this 9% return is an average overtime, meaning there will be highs and lows in market performance. Some years, your investments may exceed expectations, while other years, they might fall short. However, by focusing on the long-term average, you can plan for a retirement strategy that smooths out these fluctuations and keeps you on track.

"Half our life is spent trying to find something to do with the time we have rushed through life trying to save." – Will Rogers

The calculations take into account the compounding effect of both investment returns and inflation, providing a realistic view of how much you need to save by the time you retire. By simplifying these complex

102

financial concepts, this table helps you focus on the key figures that matter most, allowing you to plan with confidence and clarity. Whether you're 55, 60, or even 75, this approach ensures that your savings strategy is aligned with your financial goals, helping you to achieve a comfortable and secure retirement, despite the inevitable ups and downs in market performance. Here's the math to illustrate this using these assumptions:

- Desired Annual Income: $80,000
- Annual Inflation Rate adjustment: 2% ($80,000 goes to $118,875)
- Return Rate on Investments: 9%

To find the required retirement nest egg, you divide the annual income needed by the return rate:

$$\text{Required Savings} = \frac{\text{Annual Income Needed}}{\text{Return Rate}}$$

$$\text{Required Savings} = \frac{118,875}{0.09}$$

$$\text{Required Savings} \approx 1,320,833$$

This calculation shows that to generate an annual income of $118,875 with a 9% return on your money, you need a retirement nest egg of approximately $1,320,833. This method ensures that your savings are sufficient to provide a steady income throughout your retirement years, making it easier to understand and plan for your financial future. Of course, healthcare costs are the wild card that no expert can predict with a magic ball. For me, I took a position in higher education for the sole purpose of being able to purchase health care from the state as an employee between my retirement date and when Medicare kicks in at the age of 65.

Retirement Is About Clear Numbers and Financial Freedom

Ultimately, retirement is not about luck or magic; it's about understanding and working with the numbers. It's also not fuzzy math but rather simplified calculations that clearly show you where you are and where you need to be to retire comfortably. Ensuring you have a sufficient retirement nest egg is crucial, but equally important is being free from other debts such as mortgages, credit cards, car loans, student loans, or any other high-interest liabilities. Eliminating these financial burdens allows you to maximize your savings and investment returns, providing a stable and secure retirement. By focusing on these clear and practical steps, you can confidently plan for a fulfilling future where you can enjoy your retirement years without financial stress.

"It is better to live rich than to die rich." – Samuel Johnson

Finally, after all that number crunching and strategic plotting, what have we learned? Retirement isn't just about finding a cozy spot on the beach and "hoping" your bank account magically refills itself—it's about making sure you've got the cash flow to support your dreams of never setting an alarm clock again. Whether you're aiming to retire at 55 and spend your days perfecting your golf swing or you're planning to keep working just long enough to ensure you can afford that deluxe RV for cross-country adventures, the key is all in the planning.

Think of it like preparing for a marathon, but instead of running shoes and energy gels, you're stocking up on savings and investment strategies. And remember, it's not just about hitting a magic number in your retirement account—it's about making sure you've covered all your bases, from healthcare costs to those unexpected expenses (because yes, life will still throw curveballs, even when you're retired).

In the end, retirement planning is a bit like building a giant, financial safety net—one that's strong enough to catch you as you leap into the freedom of your golden years. So go ahead, dive into those spreadsheets, consult your financial advisor, and start laying the groundwork for the best part of your life. And when you finally do clock out for the last time, you can do so with the peace of mind that you've got everything under control—no magic needed, just some solid math and a well-executed plan. Cheers for that!

Chapter 16

Generating Passive Income in Retirement

Firstly, the idea of truly passive income—where money magically pours into your bank account while you sip margaritas on a beach or while you sleep—is about as real as a unicorn riding a rainbow. Sure, the concept of earning money without lifting a finger sounds dreamy, but let's be honest: every dollar you make has a string attached to some form of effort. Whether it's the sweat equity you put in at the start to get the money train rolling, the occasional elbow grease to keep it chugging along, or the inevitable panic when you need to steer it back on track, there's always some work involved. So, unless you've figured out how to train a flock of money-bearing seagulls, don't buy into the myth that you can earn big bucks while doing absolutely nothing.

"I'm always announcing my retirement. I'm still not retired."
—Dick Van Dyke

For example, real estate investments, often hyped as the holy grail of passive income, are actually more like adopting a needy pet. Sure, you might think you're just buying a property and sitting back while the rent rolls in, but before you know it, you're deep in the weeds of researching properties, wrestling with banks for financing, and playing referee-to-tenant dramas. And even if you hire a property manager to do the heavy lifting, guess who still has to make the tough calls? That's right—you. It's like thinking you've hired a dog walker, only to find out you still have to pick up the poop.

I once knew a guy who, back in 2007, bragged about owning 50 houses and claimed he was a real estate mogul. After digging a little deeper, I discovered that despite owning all those properties, he was actually losing money every month—about $5,000 in the red. When the financial crisis hit in 2007, that $5,000 deficit started to balloon, and his so-called empire quickly crumbled. If you're in the rental business and not making at least a 50% profit, even a small bump in the economy can wipe you out, leaving you with a massive financial hole and a wrecked credit score.

"I will not retire while I've still got my legs and my make-up box." —Bette Davis

Similarly, investing in stocks or bonds might sound like a set-it-and-forget-it kind of deal, but it's more like babysitting a room full of toddlers—you've got to keep an eye on them at all times. Market conditions shift faster than a sugar-crazed kid's mood, and if you're not regularly checking in, rebalancing, and staying on top of economic trends, you could end up with a big mess. Even those so-called "automated" income strategies, like dividend investing, aren't exactly hands-off. They require you to do your homework upfront and stay vigilant to ensure your investments don't go belly up.

"Well, I didn't grow up with that word 'retirement' as part of my consciousness. I didn't grow up with professionals that retired. I thought retiring was when you are tired and go to bed." —Ruby Dee

Let me tell you a little story about a person I was acquainted with, David. Dave was always on the lookout for the next big thing in the stock market. He loved reading online blogs, forums, and social media posts about hot stock tips and promising investment opportunities. One day, he stumbled upon an article raving about a company that was supposedly on the verge of skyrocketing in value. The post was full of hype, with comments from people claiming they were going "all in" on this stock, certain it was going to make them rich.

Excited by the prospect of quick gains, Dave decided to jump on the bandwagon. He poured a significant chunk of his savings into this "can't-miss" opportunity, ignoring the little voice in his head that warned him to be cautious. After all, if so many people were talking about it, it had to be good, right? Well, not quite.

As it turned out, by the time Dave heard about the stock, it was already too late. The stock had indeed surged earlier, but the buzz he was reading was from people who had bought in early and were now looking to sell off their shares to folks like Dave, who were just catching on. The price was already inflated, and when reality set in, the stock quickly plummeted back down to earth.

Dave watched in horror as his investment shrank day by day. What he didn't realize was that when a stock tip becomes common knowledge—especially when it's making the rounds on blogs and social media—most of the real opportunity is already gone. The early investors had made their profits and were getting out, leaving people like Dave holding the bag.

In the end, Dave learned a hard lesson: if you're hearing about a "great" stock opportunity from a popular source, especially online, you're probably too late to the party. The best investments are rarely the ones being shouted from the rooftops. Instead, they're the ones you research thoroughly, understanding the company, the market, and the risks before anyone else catches on. When it comes to investing, the old saying holds true: by the time you hear the news, it's often yesterday's news.

The Dream of Passive Income

The allure of passive income is all about the promise of freedom and ease—like being on a perpetual vacation where your biggest worry is what cocktail to try next. But the reality is more like a working vacation where you've still got emails to answer and meetings to attend. The truth is, generating income, whether passive or active, always involves a blend of effort, knowledge, and persistence. So, instead of chasing after a pipe dream of effortless riches, it's smarter to acknowledge that all income streams need a bit of TLC. With that mindset, you'll be ready to roll up your sleeves, do the work, and achieve lasting success—margarita optional.

Alright, let's get serious about passive income. Generating passive income involves creating streams of income that require minimal effort to maintain once established. One popular method is investing in dividend stocks, where you buy shares of companies that regularly distribute a portion of their earnings to shareholders. By researching and investing in reliable, high-dividend-yield stocks or dividend growth stocks, you can build a steady stream of income, and reinvesting dividends can further enhance growth. Real estate investments are another effective strategy, involving the purchase of property to rent out to tenants. Investing in residential or commercial properties in high-demand rental areas or Real Estate Investment Trusts (REITs) for a hands-off approach can provide substantial rental income.

> *"You can never have the comeback if you don't have the retirement."*
> —*Chael Sonnen*

Peer-to-peer lending platforms like LendingClub and Prosper allow you to lend money to individuals or small businesses in exchange for interest payments. Diversifying your loans across many borrowers can reduce risk and provide interest income from repayments. High-yield savings accounts and Certificates of Deposit (CDs) offer higher interest rates compared to traditional savings accounts, allowing you to earn more with minimal risk.

Creating a blog or YouTube channel and monetizing it through ads, sponsorships, and affiliate marketing can generate income by building an audience around a niche you are passionate about. Similarly, writing an eBook or creating an online course allows you to share your expertise and earn ongoing sales income. Publishing your eBook on platforms like Amazon Kindle or hosting your online course on sites like Udemy or Teachable can generate royalties or fees per sale/enrollment.

Developing an app or software that solves a problem or entertains users can also be lucrative. Marketing your app/software on platforms like Google Play, Apple App Store, or other marketplaces can earn you sales, subscriptions, or ad revenue. Affiliate marketing, which involves promoting other companies' products and earning a commission for every sale made through your referral link, is another viable option. Partnering with companies that offer affiliate programs and promoting their products through your blog, website, or social media can earn you commissions.

Creating an automated online business using drop shipping or print-on-demand services to fulfill orders without holding inventory can also be a profitable venture. Setting up an e-commerce site using platforms like Shopify or Etsy and automating order fulfillment can help you earn profits from sales. Earning royalties from intellectual property such as patents, trademarks, or copyrights is another method. Licensing your intellectual property to companies or individuals who will pay you royalties for using your inventions, trademarks, or creative works can provide ongoing income.

"A lot of our friends complain about their retirement. We tell 'em to get a life."
—Larry Laser

Finally, investing in a business by throwing some cash at startups or existing companies in exchange for a slice of the profit pie can be both thrilling and rewarding. It's like playing Shark Tank, but without the TV cameras and the need to perfect your dramatic pause. Platforms like AngelList let you channel your inner venture capitalist, or you can join a syndicate and feel like part of an elite club, betting on the next big thing while hoping it doesn't turn out to be the next big flop.

By dabbling in these opportunities, you can start to build a mini-empire of passive income streams—though "passive" might be a bit of a stretch when you're checking your investments like a nervous parent watching their kid's first solo bike ride. The secret sauce here is picking investments that actually interest you, match your level of expertise, and don't make you break out in a cold sweat every time you check your portfolio. And remember, reinvesting those sweet earnings is like feeding the money machine, keeping it well-oiled and ready to churn out even more dough. With a bit of savvy, a pinch of patience, and maybe a sprinkle of luck, you'll be on your way to financial stability and independence   without having to audition for a reality show.

Chapter 17

Crafting an Early Retirement Budget

For an individual with an annual income of $120,000, it is crucial to allocate funds wisely to cover necessities, discretionary spending, savings, and investments, while also accounting for taxes and health insurance. Careful planning and budgeting are essential to ensure that all aspects of your financial life are addressed, from daily living expenses to future savings goals. The following table provides a detailed monthly budget breakdown to demonstrate how to manage these income streams effectively. By following this structured approach, you can achieve financial stability and maintain a fulfilling lifestyle (see table on next page).

"Retirement is not in my vocabulary. They aren't going to get rid of me that way."
—Betty White

This structured approach helps in managing a $120,000 annual income effectively, ensuring that all essential expenses are covered while still allowing for enjoyable discretionary spending, robust savings, and responsible investment. By following a detailed budget breakdown, individuals can allocate funds to cover necessities such as housing, utilities, groceries, and transportation, as well as health insurance premiums and out-of-pocket medical expenses. Discretionary spending on activities like travel, dining out, and hobbies is also accommodated, contributing to a balanced and fulfilling lifestyle.

Moreover, this budget includes significant allocations for savings and investments, promoting long-term financial security. Contributions to retirement accounts, emergency funds, and diversified investments in stocks, bonds, and mutual funds are prioritized. This ensures that individuals are not only meeting their current financial needs but also preparing for future financial stability.

Category	%	Monthly ($)	Notes
Taxes	18%	$1,800	Taxes
Housing	15%	$1,500	Mortgage/rent
Utilities	5%	$500	Electric/Gas/Etc.
Groceries	8%	$800	Food, supplies
Transportation	5%	$500	Insurance, transport
Health Insurance	8%	$800	Medical expenses
Travel and Leisure	5%	$500	Entertainment
Socializing	5%	$500	Restaurants
Hobbies	4%	$400	Funds for activities
Savings/Retirement	20%	$2,000	IRAs, 401(k)s, Savings
Emergency Savings	5%	$500	Emergency funds
Miscellaneous	2%	$200	Emergency

The tax rate considered in this budget is the effective rate, which, after accounting for the standard deduction, reduces the nominal tax rate from 22% to an effective rate of 18%. This adjustment reflects the real tax burden more accurately, allowing for better financial planning and allocation of resources.

Regular reviews and adjustments to this budget are essential to maintaining financial health and adaptability. Personal circumstances and economic conditions can change, necessitating updates to the budget. By periodically reassessing income, expenses, and financial goals, individuals can make informed decisions to stay on track with their financial plans. This proactive approach ensures that the budget remains relevant and effective, supporting both immediate financial needs and long-term objectives. Through careful management and ongoing evaluation, a $120,000 annual income can be optimized to achieve financial stability and a rewarding retirement.

To understand how retirement savings can grow over time, it is essential to outline the underlying assumptions used in the projections. These assumptions form the foundation of the calculations and provide a framework for estimating the potential growth of retirement savings. By clearly defining these parameters, we can create a simplified model that helps illustrate how consistent contributions, growth rates, and other factors can impact long-term savings. The following table details the key assumptions that were used to generate the table showing retirement savings (*$466 per month*) growth from age 25 to 55 in 5-year increments:

Age	Annual $	Total Value
25	$5,600	$6,199
30	$5,600	$48,683
35	$5,600	$119,309
40	$5,600	$236,718
45	$5,600	$431,900
50	$5,600	$756,374
55	$5,600	$1,295,781

To effectively interpret the graph (see below) showing retirement savings growth from age 25 to 55 in 5-year increments, it is important to consider the underlying assumptions. These assumptions are the foundation for the calculations, estimating potential retirement savings accumulation. By outlining these parameters, the graph provides a simplified model that illustrates the impact of regular contributions, growth rates, and other factors on long-term savings.

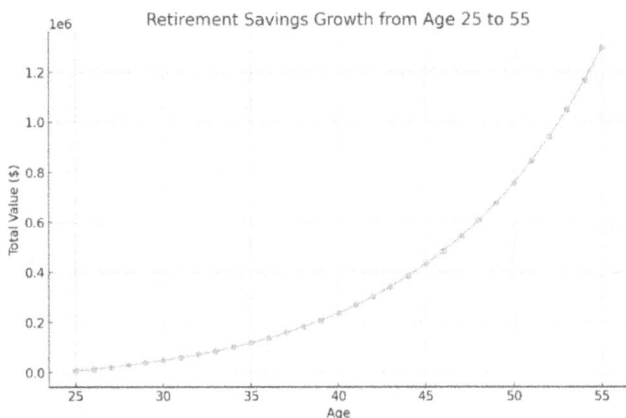

Retirement Savings Growth from Age 25 to 55

The table showing retirement savings growth from age 25 to 55 in 5-year increments is based on several key assumptions. It assumes an annual income of $70,000, with the individual contributing 8% of their income to retirement savings each year, resulting in an annual contribution of $5,600. The retirement savings are assumed to grow at an annual rate of 10.7%, with contributions and growth compounded annually. The 10.7% growth in the market reflects the historical average annual return of the S&P 500 over several decades, demonstrating the potential for substantial long-term investment gains. While this growth rate has experienced significant highs and lows, the overall average has held over time. This robust growth rate underscores the benefits of consistent, long-term investing in a diversified portfolio.

"Retirement: That's when you return from work one day and say, 'Hi, Honey,I'm home—forever.'" —Gene Perret

The individual is assumed to consistently contribute the same percentage of their income each year without any interruptions, and the annual income of $70,000 is considered to remain constant throughout the 30 years. Additionally, no withdrawals are made from the retirement savings during this time. The contributions and growth are also assumed to be tax-deferred, meaning no taxes are paid on the growth or contributions within the account until withdrawal. These assumptions provide a simplified model of how the savings could accumulate over the specified period.

The table illustrating retirement savings growth from age 25 to 55 in 5-year increments is based on several key assumptions. If the table incorporates a couple with a combined annual income of $140,000, with each person contributing 8% of their income to retirement savings annually, resulting in a combined annual contribution of $11,200. The retirement savings are projected to grow at an annual rate of 10.7%, with contributions and growth compounded annually. This 10.7% growth rate reflects the historical average annual return of the S&P 500 over several decades, showcasing the potential for significant long-term investment gains. Such robust growth underscores the advantages of consistent, long-term investing in a diversified portfolio. By the end of 30 years, this approach could potentially lead to a substantial retirement account total value of approximately $2,125,211 for the couple by age 55. This doesn't even include a company match and therefore, it is predictively low.

"I enjoy waking up and not having to go to work. So I do it three or four times a day."
—*Gene Perret*

Managing an annual income of $120,000 effectively requires a strategic approach to budgeting, saving, and investing. By allocating funds wisely across essential expenses, discretionary spending, and future savings goals, individuals can achieve both financial stability and a fulfilling lifestyle. The importance of careful planning and regular budget reviews cannot be overstated, as these practices ensure that all aspects of one's financial life are addressed, from daily living expenses to long-term retirement goals. The detailed budget breakdown provided demonstrates how to balance these income streams, ultimately paving the way for a secure financial future.

Furthermore, the projections of retirement savings growth highlight the significant impact of consistent contributions and the power of compound interest over time. By starting early and maintaining a disciplined savings strategy, individuals and couples can build a substantial nest egg by retirement age, even with a modest annual income. The assumptions used in these projections, including a 10.7% growth rate and tax-deferred contributions, illustrate the potential for long-term wealth accumulation. This underscores the importance of making informed financial decisions today to ensure a comfortable and rewarding retirement tomorrow. By following these principles, individuals can transform their income into a tool for achieving lasting financial security and independence.

Furthermore, the magic of retirement savings growth really comes down to this: consistent contributions and the sweet, sweet power of compound interest are like the dynamic duo of personal finance. Start early, stick to a savings plan, and before you know it, you're sitting on a nest egg that could hatch a golden goose by the time you retire—even if your income isn't exactly Rockefeller-level.

"My father calls acting 'a state of permanent retirement with short spurts of work."'
—Chris Pine

These projections, which include a 10.7% growth rate and the lovely tax-deferred status of your contributions, show just how much your money can grow if you treat it right. Sure, the market will have its ups and downs—it's like a roller coaster that sometimes makes you scream in excitement and other times in sheer terror—but if you stay the course, you should still be able to hit your retirement goals, not just your wildest dreams. It's like planting a money tree in your backyard—water it regularly, give it some time, and soon enough you'll be lounging in its shade, sipping piña coladas, while your neighbors are still trying to figure out how to make ends meet.

Here is just a thought about the above example, a person earning $75,000 per year often faces the same overhead costs—like housing, utilities, and groceries—as someone making $120,000 per year. The difference? The person with the lower income has much less room in their budget for saving, making it significantly harder to set aside money for retirement. This financial pressure highlights the importance of strategic planning and disciplined saving habits. Without them, the goal of a comfortable retirement can seem much more distant, even when two people have vastly different incomes. So, the challenge isn't just about how much you earn but how well you manage what you have.

The bottom line? Make smart financial decisions today, and your future self will thank you with a high-five and a one-way ticket to a beach somewhere. Turn that paycheck into a powerhouse of financial security and independence and let compound interest do the heavy lifting while you kick back and enjoy the ride!

Bucket Strategy: A Balanced Approach to Retirement

The "bucket strategy" for retirement savings is a popular approach that divides assets into different categories, or "buckets," based on when the funds will be needed and the level of risk the retiree is willing to accept. Each bucket is designed to serve a specific stage of retirement, allowing for a structured, diversified plan to cover both short-term expenses and long-term financial goals. The strategy is particularly useful in helping retirees balance the need for financial security in the early years of retirement with the need for growth to cover expenses in the later years.

Bucket 1: Short-term Needs (0-3 years)
- This bucket is for immediate or near-term expenses. It holds liquid, low-risk assets such as cash, money market funds, or short-term bonds. The goal is capital preservation and easy access to funds for living expenses in the early years of retirement.

Bucket 2: Medium-term Needs (4-10 years)
- This bucket is designed to provide income for the middle years of retirement. The funds in this bucket are invested in slightly higher-risk assets, like intermediate-term bonds, balanced funds, or conservative stock investments. The goal is to balance growth with risk management.

Bucket 3: Long-term Growth (10+ years)
- The third bucket is meant for long-term growth and is invested in higher-risk, higher-reward assets, such as stocks or equity funds. Since this bucket won't be accessed for a decade or more, it can ride out market volatility in pursuit of growth to support the later stages of retirement.

The first bucket is designated for short-term needs, typically covering the initial 0-3 years of retirement. This bucket contains liquid, low-risk assets such as cash, money market funds, or short-term bonds. The primary focus here is capital preservation, meaning the priority is to keep the money safe and easily accessible for day-to-day expenses. Since this money will be needed almost immediately, these assets mustn't be exposed to market volatility, ensuring retirees can meet their financial obligations without worrying about investment risks or market fluctuations. Having a stable, readily available source of income in this bucket provides peace of mind for retirees, knowing their immediate needs are covered.

"When a man retires, his wife gets twice as much husband for half as much money."
—*Chi Chi Rodriguez*

The second bucket is designed for medium-term needs, covering years 4-10 of retirement. The funds in this bucket are invested in moderately risky assets such as intermediate-term bonds, balanced funds, or conservative stock investments. The goal is to strike a balance between growth and risk management, allowing the money to grow modestly while minimizing exposure to large market swings. This bucket ensures that income will be available for the middle years of retirement when living expenses are still a priority, but there is some time to recover from any minor market fluctuations. By maintaining a diversified mix of assets, this bucket allows for growth while still providing a reasonable level of safety.

The third bucket focuses on long-term growth and covers the later years of retirement, typically 10 or more years into the future. This bucket is invested in higher-risk, higher-reward assets such as stocks or equity funds. Since these funds won't be needed for a decade or more, they can withstand greater market volatility in pursuit of larger returns. The aim is to provide the retiree with the growth needed to outpace inflation and ensure that there are adequate funds available for the later stages of life when healthcare costs and other unexpected expenses may arise. This bucket plays a crucial role in making sure that retirees do not outlive their savings and that they have sufficient resources to maintain their standard of living as they age.

"My retirement plan is to get thrown into a minimum security prison in Hawaii."
—Julius Sharpe

Overall, the bucket strategy is a well-rounded approach that helps retirees manage risks while ensuring they have both short-term stability and long-term growth. By structuring assets into different buckets based on time horizons, retirees can be more confident in their financial security, knowing that each stage of their retirement has been thoughtfully planned. This strategy also allows flexibility, as retirees can adjust their buckets over time, reallocating assets as needed to respond to changes in their financial situation, market conditions, or personal goals.

Using Bucket 1 to Weather Market Downturns

The **most important bucket for retirees is Bucket 1,** the short-term needs account for safeguarding your overall retirement success. This bucket acts as a crucial safety net during market downturns, holding liquid, low-risk assets such as cash, money market funds, or short-term bonds that are insulated from stock market volatility. In times of market decline, having at least three years' worth of liquid assets in this bucket allows retirees to avoid withdrawing from riskier investments, thereby preventing the need to sell stocks or other volatile assets at a loss. By relying on this stable source of funds, retirees can weather the market's fluctuations, giving riskier investments in other buckets time to recover. This strategy helps preserve long-term growth potential while ensuring immediate financial needs are met, offering both peace of mind and a more resilient financial plan during uncertain market conditions.

Chapter 18

Conclusion To Your Early Retirement

In the grand scheme of life, early retirement—or any retirement, really—is the ultimate reward for careful planning, stubborn determination, and rock-solid discipline. It's not just about dreaming big; it's about setting clear financial goals, sticking to a savings plan like your future depends on it (because it does), and resisting the temptation to veer off course every time something shiny catches your eye. Those who manage to retire comfortably aren't magicians; they're the ones who understand that a little delayed gratification goes a long way. By consistently putting their future first and not succumbing to fleeting pleasures, they turn what seems like a distant dream into a very achievable reality.

"Financial peace isn't the acquisition of stuff. It's learning to live on less than you make, so you can give money back and have money to invest. You can't win until you do this." — *Dave Ramsey*

Now, let's talk about the dark side: if you're busy chasing the latest gadgets, trying to look like a million bucks, and constantly playing the "keep up with the Joneses" game, you're setting yourself up for a lifetime sentence—of work. Sure, living beyond your means might give you a temporary high, but it's followed by a long, painful hangover of financial strain, debt, and the grim prospect of never being able to retire. Spend your life trying to look rich instead of actually building wealth, and you'll find yourself stuck on a hamster wheel, running endlessly with no finish line in sight. Meanwhile, my success speaks for itself—I'll be enjoying early retirement at 55.5 years old while my friends, colleagues, and associates keep working into their 60s, all because they were more focused on looking successful than actually being successful.

Remember, true success isn't about flashy appearances; it's about achieving real freedom from the grind, living life on your own terms, and escaping the endless cycle of work and obligation.

Trust me, you will thank you for it in the future!

One last quest from a Financial Guru................

"You are responsible for valuing yourself and stating that value to the world. This holds equally true for employees of companies large and small as well as artists and stay-at-home moms."
— Suze Orman

Bibliography

Bankrate. (2021). FIRE movement: Financial Independence, Retire Early explained. Retrieved from https://www.bankrate.com/retirement/fire-movement/

Bankrate. (2023). Avoiding bank fees. Retrieved from Bankrate

Bengen, W. P. (1994). Determining withdrawal rates using historical data. Journal of Financial Planning, 7(4), 171-180.

Bogle, J. C. (2017). The Little Book of Common-Sense Investing. Wiley.

CarsDirect. (2023). Leasing vs. Buying a Car: Which Is Best for You? Retrieved from https://www.carsdirect.com/

CNET. (2023). When to upgrade your electronics. Retrieved from CNET

College Board. (2023). Trends in college pricing 2023. Retrieved from https://reports.collegeboard.org/trends/college-pricing

Consumer Financial Protection Bureau. (2023). Credit card interest. Retrieved from CFPB

Consumer Reports. (2022). Lease vs. Buy a Car: How to Decide. Retrieved from Consumer Reports

Cooley, P. L., Hubbard, C. M., & Walz, D. T. (1998). Retirement savings: Choosing a withdrawal rate that is sustainable. AAII Journal, 20(2), 16-21.

CNBC. (2021, October 8). Does the 4% rule for retirement withdrawals still work? Retrieved from https://www.cnbc.com/2021/10/08/does-the-4percent-rule-for-retirement-withdrawals-still-work.html

CNBC. (2023). Lottery ticket spending. Retrieved from CNBC

Debt.org. (2024). Debt in America: Statistics and demographics. Retrieved from https://www.debt.org/

Dittmar, H. (2008). Consumer Culture, Identity and Well-Being: The Search for the 'Good Life' and the 'Body Perfect'. Psychology Press.

Early Retirement Extreme: http://earlyretirementextreme.com

Edmunds. (2023). Buying vs. Leasing a Car: Pros and Cons. Retrieved from Edmunds

Employee Benefit Research Institute. (2021). 2021 Retirement Confidence Survey. Retrieved from https://www.ebri.org/retirement/retirement-confidence-survey.

Energy.gov. (2023). Energy-saving tips. Retrieved from Energy.gov

Federal Reserve. (2023). Household Debt and Credit Report. Retrieved from https://www.federalreserve.gov/

Ferri, R. A. (2016). All About Asset Allocation. McGraw-Hill Education.

Fidelity Investments. (2020). The road to early retirement: Insights on achieving financial independence. Retrieved from https://www.fidelity.com/viewpoints/retirement/early-retirement.

Fidelity. (2021). Is the 4% rule still valid? Retrieved from https://www.fidelity.com/viewpoints/retirement/4-percent-rule

Financial Samurai. (2023, September 12). Suze Orman is right. You need $5 million or more to retire early. Financial Samurai. https://www.financialsamurai.com/suze-orman-is-right-you-need-5-million-or-more-to-retire-early/#:~:text=Suze%20Orman%20is%20right.,amount%20of%20risk%2Dadjusted%20income

Forbes Advisor. (2023). How to save on insurance. Retrieved from Forbes Advisor

Hoffman, J. (2022). Healthcare Options for Early Retirees. Penguin Random House.

Hester, T. (2019). Work Optional: Retire Early the Non-Penny-Pinching Way. Little, Brown Spark.

Investopedia. (2024). Four percent rule. Retrieved from https://www.investopedia.com/terms/f/four-percent-rule.asp

IRS. (2023). Retirement Topics - IRA Contribution Limits. Internal Revenue Service.

Investopedia. (2023). How much does a daily coffee habit cost? Retrieved from Investopedia

Kasser, T. (2002). The High Price of Materialism. MIT Press.

Kiplinger. (2023). The 4% rule is dead, long live the 4% rule. Retrieved from https://www.kiplinger.com/retirement/retirement-planning/602539/the-4-rule-is-dead-long-live-the-4-rule

Kiyosaki, R. T. (2011). Rich Dad Poor Dad. Plata Publishing.

Kobliner, B. (2017). Get a Financial Life: Personal Finance in Your Twenties and Thirties. Simon & Schuster.

LendingTree. (2024). Mortgage Statistics: 2024. Retrieved from LendingTree.com

Money Crashers. (2023). High-end fashion spending. Retrieved from Money Crashers

Mr. Money Mustache, 2024. Retrieved August 23, 2024.
https://www.mrmoneymustache.com

MyMoney.gov. (2024). Consumer Expenditure Survey Overview.
Retrieved August 23, 2024, from
https://www.mymoney.gov/node/97053

National Center for Education Statistics. (2023). Student financial aid
data. Retrieved from
https://nces.ed.gov/programs/digest/d21/tables/dt21_331.95.as
p

National Restaurant Association. (2021). Restaurant industry statistics.
Retrieved from National Restaurant Association

NerdWallet. (2023). Unused gym memberships. Retrieved from
NerdWallet

NerdWallet. (2024). The 4% rule: What is it and how does it work?
Retrieved from https://www.nerdwallet.com/article/investing/4-
rule-retirement

O'Leary, K. (2018). The Simple Path to Wealth. Independent Publisher.

Orman, S. (2016). The Money Book for the Young, Fabulous & Broke.
Riverhead Books.

Pew Research Center. (2021). Retiree finances: How Americans are saving
and preparing for retirement. Retrieved from
https://www.pewresearch.org/fact-tank/2021/11/03/retiree-
finances-how-americans-are-saving-and-preparing-for-retirement/

Piketty, T. (2014). Capital in the Twenty-First Century. Harvard
University Press.

Politico. (2024). Debt-burdened Americans find no reprieve even as
inflation cools. Retrieved from https://www.politico.com/

Ramsey, D. (2013). The Total Money Makeover. Thomas Nelson.

Ramsey Solutions. (2024). 10 Characteristics of debt-free living. Retrieved
from https://www.ramseysolutions.com/

Robin, V. (2019). Your Money or Your Life: 9 Steps to Transforming
Your Relationship with Money and Achieving Financial
Independence. Penguin Books.

Roth, J. (2019). Your Money: The Missing Manual. O'Reilly Media.

Sabin, D. (2020). Side Hustle: From Idea to Income in 27 Days. Currency.

Schor, J. B. (1998). The Overspent American: Why We Want What We
Don't Need. Harper Perennial.

Statista. (2022). Subscription economy statistics. Retrieved from Statista

The Balance. (2023). What is the 4% rule? Retrieved from
https://www.thebalance.com/what-is-the-4-rule-2388824

The Institute for College Access & Success (TICAS). (2023). Student debt
and the class of 2023. Retrieved from
https://ticas.org/reports/student-debt-and-the-class-of-2023/

The FIRE Movement, 2024. Retrieved from https://www.choosefi.com

The New York Times. (2018). How to Retire in Your 30s With $1 Million
in the Bank. Retrieved from
https://www.nytimes.com/2018/09/01/style/fire-financial-
independence-retire-early.html

University of California Office of the President. (2023). Annual report on
student financial aid and debt. Retrieved from
https://www.ucop.edu/institutional-research-academic-
planning/_files/factsheets/2023/uc-student-debt.pdf

U.S. Bureau of Labor Statistics. (2022). Consumer Expenditures - 2021.
Retrieved from BLS website

U.S. Bureau of Labor Statistics. (2024). Consumer Expenditure Survey.
U.S. Department of Labor. Retrieved August 23, 2024, from
https://www.bls.gov/cex/

Vanderkam, L. (2015). I Know How She Does It: How Successful
Women Make the Most of Their Time. Penguin Random House.

Vanguard. (2021). How America saves 2021: Retirement saving in the U.S.
Retrieved from
https://pressroom.vanguard.com/nonindexed/How-America-
Saves-2021.pdf.

www.ingramcontent.com/pod-product-compliance
Lightning Source LLC
Chambersburg PA
CBHW071705210326
41597CB00017B/2344